THE GREAT PROPERTY FALLACY

In this groundbreaking book, Frank Upham uses empirical analysis and economic theory to demonstrate how myths surrounding property law have blinded us to our own past and led us to demand that developing countries implement policies that are mistaken and impossible. Starting in the sixteenth century with the English enclosures and ending with the World Bank's recent attempt to reform Cambodian land law – while moving through nineteenth-century America, postwar Japan, and contemporary China – Upham dismantles the virtually unchallenged assertion that growth cannot occur without stable legal property rights and shows how rapid growth can come only through the destruction of preexisting property structures and their replacement by more productive ones. He argues persuasively for the replacement of Western myths and theoretical simplifications with nuanced approaches to growth and development that are sensitive to complexity and difference and responsive to the political and social factors essential to successful broad-based development.

Frank K. Upham is the Wilf Family Professor of Property Law at New York University School of Law. He teaches Property, Law and Development, and various courses on Japanese and Chinese law and society. His book, *Law and Social Change in Postwar Japan*, won the Thomas J. Wilson Prize from Harvard University Press. In addition to having taught property law for over thirty years at several American law schools, he has taught in Argentina, China, Israel, Japan, and Taiwan. Upham has also worked as a World Bank consultant on the reform of property law in Southeast Asia.

The Great Property Fallacy

THEORY, REALITY, AND GROWTH IN DEVELOPING COUNTRIES

FRANK K. UPHAM
New York University School of Law

CAMBRIDGE
UNIVERSITY PRESS

CAMBRIDGE
UNIVERSITY PRESS

University Printing House, Cambridge CB2 8BS, United Kingdom

One Liberty Plaza, 20th Floor, New York, NY 10006, USA

477 Williamstown Road, Port Melbourne, VIC 3207, Australia

314-321, 3rd Floor, Plot 3, Splendor Forum, Jasola District Centre, New Delhi - 110025, India

79 Anson Road, #06-04/06, Singapore 079906

Cambridge University Press is part of the University of Cambridge.

It furthers the University's mission by disseminating knowledge in the pursuit of education, learning and research at the highest international levels of excellence.

www.cambridge.org
Information on this title: www.cambridge.org/9781108422833
DOI: 10.1017/9781108525381

First published 2018

A catalogue record for this publication is available from the British Library

Library of Congress Cataloging in Publication data

NAMES: Upham, Frank K., author.
TITLE: The great property fallacy : theory, reality, and growth in developing countries / Frank K. Upham, New York University School of Law.
DESCRIPTION: First Edition. | Cambridge, United Kingdom ; New York, NY, USA : Cambridge University Press, 2018 | Includes bibliographical references and index.
IDENTIFIERS: LCCN 2017042283| ISBN 9781108422833 (hardback) | ISBN 9781108436946 (paperback)
SUBJECTS: LCSH: Right of property--Economic aspects. | Law and economic development. | Law and economics. | BISAC: LAW / General.
CLASSIFICATION: LCC K721.5 .U64 2018 | DDC 346/.124043–dc23
LC record available at https://lccn.loc.gov/2017042283

ISBN 978-1-108-42283-3 Hardback
ISBN 978-1-108-43694-6 Paperback

For Leslie

Contents

Preface

This book comes out of the confluence of my teaching and scholarship. I began teaching American property law over thirty years ago, not because of any interest in the subject, but because first-year Property was the course that Ohio State College of Law needed me to teach. I enjoyed teaching Property but my scholarship was focused on comparative law and specifically Japan and later China. Two developments in the late 1980s brought these parallel tracks into contact. First was the economic growth of China without a robust legal system. Second was the "second law and development movement" stimulated by the World Bank's adoption of neo-institutional economics and its focus on legal institutions as a prerequisite to growth. The immediate catalyst was a World Bank consultancy to the Lao People's Democratic Republic (PDR) to lecture on the reform of Laotian land law. I was not the Bank's first choice. They had appropriately hired someone with greater scholarly accomplishments in property law and especially in civilian property law. That person withdrew at the last minute, however, so I went in his stead.

I was allowed to structure the lectures on my own with two exceptions: I was to stress that land must be privately owned and that any land taken by eminent domain was to be compensated with the fair market value of the land. I was also, less formally, asked not to use the People's Republic of China (PRC) as a model for Laotian reforms. I was puzzled by these restrictions for several reasons. First, of course, was the fact that China was already the leading recent example of rapid economic growth. It was also, unlike, e.g., France, a foreign country whose land law I knew something about, but I was not so naïve that I did not understand (or think I understood) why the World Bank did not want China to be Lao's model. More troubling was the substance. Neither individualized private ownership of land nor fair market value compensation seemed to me to be necessary to growth or development. Indeed, America's own experience, much less that of China or Vietnam, contradicted both stipulations, and the ideological transformation that either would require of the Laotian government seemed too much to ask of a very poor country and irrelevant in terms of growth and development. Nonetheless, I toed the line. The World Bank was my client, it had great depths of expertise in the area, and it was paying me well.

After the end of my consultancy, I began to pay attention to the discourse around international development efforts with particular interest in what type of property law was said to be necessary for growth to occur. I discovered that even more than individual private property and conformity to market principles, the most consistently and confidently repeated prescription for growth was the need for formal, stable property rights. I was struck by the direct contradiction to much of what I teach first-year law students, which is not how courts preserve property rights but how they and legislatures legitimately change them. By this time, I was also becoming interested in the relative lack of formal law and courts in Chinese growth and development. Both my teaching and scholarship, therefore, led me to the conclusion that contemporary development practice did not match and, indeed, contradicted the historical experience of the societies with which I am most familiar and which represent the world's most economically successful societies. Instead of learning from actual experience, it appeared to me, development professionals were urging poor countries to adopt an imagined and idealized version of Western property systems that have never actually existed anywhere.

I decided to look more closely at the theory of economic development to see if the discrepancy had come out of economists' different understanding of the nature of property rights. I began with Harold Demsetz's story of the Montagne Indians, which is standard fare for American property courses. A more conscientious reading of Demsetz, however, only deepened the mystery because the moral of the Montagne story is the need to change, not preserve property rights. I then moved on to the larger economic theory within which Demsetz resides, neo-institutional economics and, specifically, the work of Douglass North. Far from clarifying matters, however, the mystery deepened since North too is all about change, not stasis. Furthermore, he points out forcefully the political contingency of any set of property rights, bringing into question another staple of development rhetoric: the need for apolitical, independent courts, what was often referred to as a rule of law system. Since American common law courts have been anything but apolitical, I was again struck by the otherworldly nature of the legal side of current development rhetoric and practice, and realized that the gap was not just between practice and experience but also between practice and economic theory.

This book is the result of my attempt to understand this anomaly.

Acknowledgments

The research and writing of this book was supported by the Filomen D'Agostino and Max E. Greenberg Research Fund at New York University (NYU) School of Law and by the gift of the Wilf Family Chair in Property Law.

I am very grateful to the scores of students who have done research on one or more of the topics covered in this book. I want to thank three specifically: Mizuki Koshimoto, Leah Trzcinski, and Gabriele Wadlig. Each of them was indispensable to the book.

I have benefited immeasurably from my colleagues at NYU and elsewhere, including participants at several workshops where I presented my ideas to critical but supportive audiences. I am particularly grateful to Professor Yuka Kaneko of the Graduate School of International Cooperation Studies, Kobe University. Special thanks go to those who read parts or all of early versions of the manuscript: Daniel Fitzpatrick, Jedidiah Kroncke, Natalie Lichtenstein, Lance Liebman, William Nelson, Shitong Qiao, Michael Trebilcock, David Trubek, Katrina Wyman, and especially my friend and pro bono editor, Rob Evans.

1

Introduction

This book is about the role of property law in development. It challenges the ubiquitous and rarely questioned assertion that legal property rights are necessary to economic growth and argues that this view is incomplete, misleading, and dangerous. It is incomplete because economic growth can and has occurred without property rights. It is misleading because it implies that property rights *per se* will invariably contribute to economic growth when in fact the role of property rights in growth is contingent on the surrounding social, political, and technological context. It is dangerous because a failure to recognize the complexity of property rights will mislead policymakers in their attempts to bring the world's poorest people out of poverty.

The faith in legal property rights emerged from neo-institutional economics, particularly from the work of Ronald Coase, Harold Demsetz, and Douglass North and their emphasis on the necessity of certain social structures for productive investment and exchange. They took a broad view of the types of institutions needed, as have many legal scholars.[1] They expressly included custom and community norms, but the practitioners who later turned theory into policy narrowed the focus to the formal institutions of the legal system: legal rights found in statutes or judicial opinions and defined, amended, and enforced by courts and other institutions working under legislative and

[1] See respectively Ronald H. Coase, "The Problem of Social Cost," *Journal of Law & Economics* 3 (1960): 1; Harold Demsetz, "Toward a Theory of Property Rights," *The American Economic Review* 57 (1967) 347; and Douglass North, *Institutions, Institutional Change and Economic Performance* (Cambridge: Cambridge University Press, 1981) and Douglass North, *Structure and Change in Economic History* (New York: Norton, 1990). Notable examples of legal scholars approaching institutions broadly include Robert C. Ellickson, *Order without Law: How Neighbors Settle Disputes*, (Cambridge: Harvard University Press, 1994), and Michael Trebilcock, "Communal Property Rights: The Papua New Guinean Experience," *University of Toronto Law Journal* 34 (1984): 377.

judicial authority.[2] In doing so, these policymakers ignored the broader early approach and distorted the basic theory, but this focus on formal norms and institutions supported by rule of law rhetoric has nonetheless been ubiquitous since the 1980s. It has provided the policy justification for spending hundreds of millions of dollars on legal reform and formed the intellectual foundation for advice given by virtually all agencies and nongovernmental organizations (NGOs) of all political stripes engaged in development assistance across the globe. Not only has much of this investment been wasted, but the results have often destabilized existing property regimes and left societies worse off.[3]

This book addresses this theoretical and policy failure empirically by examining the experiences of societies from sixteenth-century England to twenty-first-century Cambodia. The goal is not to deny property's importance but to deepen our understanding of its social roles throughout history: to better understand how we conceptualize it; how in diverse cultures property has been created, operationalized, manipulated, and destroyed; and how development practitioners' fixation on property as formal legal rights can lead us astray.

Their fixation is understandable. The translation of the seemingly opaque and inefficient social structures of poor countries into clear legal rules and institutions can make the task of shaping developing countries' societies from the outside at least plausible, if still far from easy. If secure entitlements emerge primarily from the formal system as rights, they can be understood by anyone with legal knowledge and transferred from one society to another through expertise, financial resources, and political will. Focusing on formal law, in other words, allows one to shift one's gaze comfortably from social complexity to the seductive elegance of Demsetzian transaction costs and Coasian bargaining.

The problem, of course, is that empirical reality rests in complexity – which Demsetz, Coase, and North all recognized – and social experience with property has rarely fit the elegance of our projections. Instead, as we shall see, the vigorous enforcement of property rights can, in certain circumstances, prevent rapid economic growth rather than foster it, and the best-practices

2 Rhetoric such as the following by the Chief Counsel of the World Bank's Legal and Judicial Reform Practice Group is typical: "A free and robust market can thrive only ... where individual freedoms and property rights are accorded respect and where redress for violations of such rights can be found in fair and equitable courts." Maria Dakolias, "A Strategy for Judicial Reform: The Experience in Latin America," *Virginia Journal of International Law* 36 (1995–1996): 167, 168.

3 See Daniel Fitzpatrick, "Evolution and Chaos in Property Rights Systems: The Third World Tragedy of Contested Access," *Yale Law Journal* 115 (2006): 996.

form of global expertise often fails when it encounters local circumstances. Failure to meet social scientists' dreams would not be so bad in itself, but there is more at stake. The effort to transform the superficially chaotic norms of a poor country into a coherent, transparent, and open network often destroys preexisting social arrangements invisible to best-practices expertise. What is left is not a replication of the practices of developed countries, but a mixture of old and new, bottom-up and top-down, foreign and indigenous normative structures that all too often fails to deliver social progress or economic growth.

At the core of my argument are two simple assumptions: First, that the level of economic production at a specific time and place depends on the technology available and the incentives for its utilization and, second, that the politically powerful will tend to preserve the social structures most valuable to their own interests. Over the past several centuries, the paradigmatic means of such protection has been a formal legal system with property entitlements designed to preserve the status quo, which is entirely unobjectionable as long as stability remains the goal. Once rapid growth becomes the goal, however, fundamental change becomes necessary and it is rarely easy, especially if the inevitable losers can draw on property rights to protect their interests.[4] What distinguishes property from other legal rights, after all, is that they provide their owner with power over a resource that can be enforced without reference to relative social value. And it is not simply a question of wealth, which in theory could be redistributed to assuage the losers. Attachment to the status quo does not end with its material benefits. Observers of capitalism from Karl Marx to Joseph Schumpeter to Douglass North have long recognized the tendency of elites to resist socially beneficial change. As Karl Polanyi put it, "[T]he interests of a class most directly refer to standing and rank, to status and security, that is, they are primarily not economic but social."[5] It is not, in other words, only the impossibility of perfect bargaining that can prevent beneficial change within the existing structure of existing property rights; it is also the desire to retain political power and social status.

It should not be surprising, therefore, that the peacetime destruction of property rights has usually been incremental, rarely straightforward, and virtually always cloaked in obfuscating rhetoric. It has nonetheless proceeded

4 Ronald Coase himself recognized that massive transaction costs frequently overwhelm both voluntary exchange and political bargaining. *See* minutes 37 to 43 of the 17th Annual Coase Lecture by Ronald Coase at the University of Chicago, April 1, 2003, available at www.law.uchicago.edu/video/coase040103.

5 Karl Polanyi, *The Great Transformation* (New York: Rineholt, 1957), 153. See North, *Structure and Change*, 180–4, for a discussion of Marx, Schumpeter, and Polanyi on the importance of ideology and the ideological alienation arguably caused by capitalism.

throughout history. Sometimes it has been in response to and productive of normative change, and in Chapter 4 we examine the elimination of the property rights and social status of Japanese landlords to build post-World War II democracy. The destruction of property rights for economic reasons is more central to our concerns, however, and perhaps more surprising, given that property is the very institution that the development canon would have us rely on to produce economic growth. In the case studies of Chapters 3, 5, and 6, therefore, we examine four instances of the destruction of property rights: the elimination of sixteenth-century English villagers' rights to enter their lord's land to allow monoculture and sheep pasturage; the nineteenth-century narrowing of American farmers' right to clean water to accommodate industrialization; the late twentieth-century elimination of Chinese villagers' share of communal production to force market production; and the twenty-first-century dispossession of Cambodian subsistence farmers and small entrepreneurs to make way for more commercially productive large-scale development.

Each of these stories raises important questions about the moral, political, and social costs of economic growth, but both the contemporaneous political rhetoric justifying these changes and the later scholarship analyzing them rarely recognize that property rights have been destroyed.[6] Demsetz in his iconic 1967 account of the Montagne Indians' individualization of communal hunting grounds talked of the "emergence" and "development" of individualized rights.[7] More recently, Daron Acemoglu and James Robinson praised the "rationalizing" of "archaic forms of property rights" after England's Glorious Revolution of 1688.[8] They make no mention of what happened to the preexisting property rights or their owners. On the contrary, Acemoglu and Robinson speak approvingly of the "steadfast enforcement" or "strengthening" of property rights in the very same paragraph in which they extoll their "rationalization" or "reorganization."[9] It is as if these new "rational" rights appear spontaneously without political action and without affecting existing interests or, equally implausible, as if the beneficiaries of the prior regime graciously yield their "archaic" legal entitlements and the political power, social status, and economic rents they represent in order for the society to make net social gains.

6 The process has not been completely unnoticed. See, e.g., Stuart Banner, "Transitions Between Property Regimes," *Journal of Legal Studies* 31 (2002): S359.

7 Demsetz, "Theory," 350.

8 Daron Acemoglu and James Robinson, *Why Nations Fail: The Origins of Power, Prosperity, and Poverty* (New York: Random House, 2012), 102–3.

9 Ibid., 198–9.

This consistent avoidance of talk of the destruction of property rights is not an oversight. Hypocrisy, sophistry, and euphemism are integral and necessary devices for the moral and political legitimation of the pain of rapid economic growth. None of the property rights changes this book explores was prevented: English fields were enclosed; American streams were dammed and polluted; Japanese landlords were dispossessed and sent to the trash heap of history; Chinese commune members were set free to produce for the market or go hungry; and Cambodian villagers are being transformed from subsistence farmers to agricultural laborers. Each change caused pain as large numbers of people who did not have the political power to protect their interests had their expectations of a stable life frustrated,[10] but each change (with the possible exception of the ongoing process in Cambodia) also led either to increased productivity or deepened democracy and dramatic gains in net social welfare.

Analogous processes are occurring or should be occurring in poor countries today, and one role of social science scholarship should be to understand and describe how net beneficial change can occur as quickly, efficiently, and justly as possible and to generalize from those success stories. Unfortunately, fundamental social change and the transformation of legal structures that accompany and facilitate it are rarely easy or straightforward. Each instance is different and our understanding, particularly in the development context, is complicated by the natural tendency to search for technical fixes that can be transferred easily from one society to the next. That quest for best practices is futile, however, at least in the sense of providing fail-safe policies on the ground. Human society is too complex, but the impossibility of finding universal explanations for broad social questions does not make understanding past

[10] The overwhelming gain in productivity that followed Chinese reforms may lead the observer to overlook the effect on those ill-equipped to produce for a market economy. The difficulty of the adjustment spawned a genre of post-Maoist literature in the late 1970s and early 1980s known as Reform literature. While recognizing the increased wealth and individual freedom, it stressed both the loss of material security for the weak and the normative impact on society as a whole, as an excerpt from the description of the start of one such novel, *The Descendants of Lu*, portrays:

> The Little Carpenter's opening his own carpenter workshop is predicated upon the disintegration of the collective workshop, which does not mean emancipation for everyone. To Fu Kuan, whose laboring capacity is weak and who has a large family to feed, this is a disaster. And more importantly, this brings crisis to the traditional ethics of mutual aid and equality and the socialist ethics.

Jun Xie, "The Wild Individual: Politics and Aesthetics of Realism in Post-Mao China" (PhD dissertation, New York University, 2016), 216. The similar effect of the privatization of state-owned enterprises is dramatically captured in Zhang Meng's movie, *Gang de Qin* (English title, *The Piano in a Factory*).

experience any less vital to coping with the future. This book tries to increase that understanding by examining the range of roles that property rights have played in the growth and development of a range of societies. As we shall see, they have, variously, slowed the process of change, legitimated it, served as the very agent of change, done all three at once, and sometimes played virtually no role at all.

Because the role of property in development has been complex and contradictory, it is important to define my terms and to note what I do not claim. Like the law reform practitioners whom I criticize, I define property rights as *legal* entitlements and exclude the political, social, and ideological structures included by North et al. I don't deny that human beings, whether individual farmers or multinational corporations, require assurance, formal or informal, that they will be able to reap a reasonable return on their investment before they will expend time, labor, or capital. I don't deny that top-down, externally imposed formalization may produce growth. The dispossession of North American and Australian indigenous peoples by European settlers' property regimes are certainly examples, and the account in Chapter 6 of the replacement of existing Cambodian land rights by a new land law created by the World Bank may be another.

My point, therefore, is not that such growth can never be desirable from the perspective of aggregate wealth but simply that it will almost invariably eliminate existing social structures. Nor do I claim that property rights, even narrowly defined as judicially enforceable rules, are only desirable for economic growth. Indeed, one of the cornerstones of development, as opposed to growth, is the re-creation of stable property rights after periods of change. Even in countries desperately in need of rapid growth such as late twentieth-century China and contemporary Cambodia, property rights can play an important role in the achievement of social justice. But as we will see in the chapters that follow, they can also be an obstacle to the structural changes that will contribute to prosperity and progress.

THE STRUCTURE OF THE BOOK

Chapter 2 sets the stage for the case studies by tracing the emergence of neo-institutional economics founded by Coase, Demsetz, North, and others. It foregrounds their most basic insight, one honored more in the breach than in the observance: the need for institutional change when societies are faced with normative or technological opportunities or threats. It emphasizes that these economists recognized informal as well as formal means of creating, maintaining, and modifying property, and understood that entitlements can be protected by social norms, community customs, and political bargaining as well as through legislation and litigation. It then shows how the recognition of both the need to adjust incentive structures – which, in the interest of avoiding euphemism, I call the destruction of property rights – and the importance of both legal and nonlegal mechanisms in that destruction has largely disappeared as the attention to institutions migrated from Demsetz and North to development economics more generally and eventually to global legal reformers.

Against the theoretical backdrop in Chapter 2, Chapter 3 describes how two societies, different in time and space, adjusted existing property rights in response to market opportunities. It examines the slow-motion destruction of villagers' property rights during the more than three centuries of the English enclosure movement and the nineteenth-century narrowing of American farmers' right to clean water. In England, the lords first used legal institutions to dispossess their fellow villagers, then legal rhetoric to legitimate the result, but what makes the enclosures iconic in legal history is that commoners used the same legal system to delay and sometimes frustrate the process, eventually stretching it over centuries. That the powerful could use law to oppress the weak should not be news; that the weak could use law to resist has been seen as an initial step not only toward modern law, but also in the development of democracy itself.[11] In the American instance, the law, instead of delaying the dispossession of the weak by the strong, became the mechanism by which emerging industrial interests destroyed the property rights of the dominant agrarian classes. Both cases qualify, in Polanyi's terms, as "revolutions of the rich against the poor."[12] In both instances, the destruction of legal entitlements allowed new technologies to take advantage of market opportunities.

Chapter 4 turns to a case that is quite the reverse: land reform in post-World War II Japan. Here, reform took land from the rural elite and gave it to their tenants and it was politics, not market forces, that drove the change. Neither the land reform itself nor the agricultural policy that has maintained small-scale independent family farmers ever since was designed to increase agricultural efficiency and production, and in this respect, there have been no surprises. Japanese agricultural policy has not made anyone rich, least of all the consumers of Japan. What links these three case studies, therefore, is neither the political direction of legal change nor the relationship between the

[11] See, for example, Barrington Moore, Jr., *Social Origins of Dictatorship and Democracy: Lord and Peasant in the Making of the Modern World* (New York: Beacon, 1967); E. P. Thompson, *The Making of the English Working Class* (New York: Vintage, 1963); and Polanyi, *Great Transformation*, on the long-term political effect of the enclosures.

[12] Polanyi, *Great Transformation*, 35.

law and market opportunity, but the manipulation of law to destroy property rights in the service of social change.

Chapter 5 turns to an entirely different case, post-reform China, which demonstrates that economic growth is possible in the absence of formal property rights. While China has been constructing a "rule of law with Chinese characteristics" for more than thirty years, formal legal institutions have rarely played the conventional role of providing the security of investment that economic growth demands and perhaps even less in legitimating the changes in property allocation that have stimulated and facilitated growth. Yet China has created precisely the kind of vibrant, deep, and broad markets that most economists and development practitioners insist can develop and function only with the formal legal institutions that China largely lacked during this period.

Although China's stunning success has directly contradicted the conventional wisdom, law and development experts have largely ignored it, as the story of Cambodian land law reform, recounted in Chapter 6, demonstrates. The chapter examines two projects, the Boeung Kak Lake real estate development and the creation of the Koh Kong Sugar Plantation, which involve, respectively, prime Phnom Penh real estate and remote agricultural land. In each case, despite the elaborate, best-practices planning and control exerted by foreign experts, residents' long-standing rights to land were ignored and statutory language was manipulated to facilitate the transfer of the land to more powerful and ostensibly more productive users. As the chapter shows, the implementation of the Land Law did not realize its creators' dreams, but may, nonetheless, result in accelerated economic growth, if not development as more broadly conceived.

TWO LESSONS

A set of case studies can only prove so much, whereas quantitative methodologies and rankings can *appear* to prove a great deal, even when the data on which they're based are acknowledged to be flawed or nonexistent and the resulting models ambiguous or misleading.[13] Of course, a World Bank or

[13] See discussion of Daniel Kaufmann et al., *Governance Matters*, 21 (World Bank Institute, Policy Research Working Paper No. 2196, 1999), in Frank K. Upham, "From Demsetz to Deng: Speculations on the Implications of Chinese Growth for Law and Development Theory," *Journal of International Law and Politics* 41 (2009): 551–602, 558–9. See also Daniel Berkowitz, Katharina Pistor, and Jean-Francois Richard, "Economic development, legality, and the transplant effect," *European Economic Review* 47.1 (2003): 165–95. For an excuse, if not justification, for the use of admittedly incomplete and inaccurate models, see Paul Krugman, "The Fall and Rise of Development Economics," http://web.mit.edu/krugman/www/dishpan.html: "The problem is that there is no alternative to models. We all think in

USAID official trying to choose between two possible loan recipients needs both information to help make the decision and authority to justify it. The numbers produced by quantitative methodologies can appear to produce both; case studies only the former. But case studies are ideal when we need not to oversimplify and take for granted presumed universal truths but to deconstruct and complicate them. The book concludes in Chapter 7 by doing precisely that.

The book does not offer the kind of general but abstract insight into social structure found in Coase's *The Problem of Social Cost* or Demsetz's *Toward a Theory of Property Rights*. Instead, it uses the comparative and historical data of the case studies to deepen our real-life understanding of the role of property and property rights in changing societies. From its examination of the actual roles of formal legal institutions in five disparate contexts two critical lessons emerge. The first is that formal property rights are not the simple and straightforward drivers of economic progress portrayed in World Bank literature or Hernando de Soto's *The Other Path*. On the contrary, they are deeply complex in nature and have played a wide variety of social, political, and economic functions in recent history. Their enforcement has slowed economic growth and stimulated political development; their destruction has facilitated growth and legitimated governmental theft; they have favored the powerful, but they have also mitigated the pain of adjustment for the weak; and in some instances they have played virtually no role at all. The deeper lesson is that pat generalizations of their role in a specific instance are not only likely to be wrong but also, and more importantly, may produce unexpected and undesired results.

The second critical lesson extends beyond property law to the "rule of law movement" more generally: legal reform is invariably political. Theoretical certainty and a naïve faith in the objectivity and rationality of technical knowledge drive contemporary law and development practice. But the belief that a computerized land registry based on a satellite-created cadastral survey will create the same land market in Cambodia as in Australia, for example, defies human experience. Too often, such utopian beliefs drive rule-of-law advocates to treat formal legal institutions as the only means by which developing societies can effectively create and protect economic assets, regulate markets, resolve disputes, and foster productive exchange. As a consequence, vast amounts of time, money, and expertise are wasted attempting to establish first-world legal systems where they are unlikely to thrive and may well displace preexisting normative orders that might be more suitable to the

simplified models, all the time. The sophisticated thing to do is not to pretend to stop, but to be self-conscious – to be aware that your models are maps rather than reality."

complicated tasks of economic growth and political progress. In other words, instead of focusing on the universal aspirations of our dreams for legal systems, we should be willing to deal with the messy and unsatisfying variety and complexity of law's historical role in growth and development. In doing so, we can give depth to the cliché that "one size does not fit all" when it comes to legal reform and provide a cautionary note as we consider policies for poor countries in the future.

2

Physics Envy

Property Rights in Development Theory

The history of development economics begins with the end of World War II. The emergence of scores of newly independent nations coupled with the Cold War and the urgent need to gain those nations' political and military allegiance caught Western economists off guard. Up to that point, economics had been focused on market equilibrium among Western nations and was unconcerned with growth in our contemporary sense of poor nations getting rich. Economists in industrialized nations, as one development economics textbook puts it, "had no readily available conceptual apparatus with which to analyze the process of economic growth in largely agrarian societies characterized by the virtual absence of modern economic structures."[1] Nor did they have any knowledge, data, or experience in poor countries. What they did have was their own experience and familiarity with the economic history

[1] Michael P. Todaro and Stephen C. Smith, *Economic Development* (London: Pearson Ninth Edition, 2006), 104. Indeed, economic growth itself is relatively new. As economists James M. Cypher and James L. Dietz put it in their textbook *The Process of Economic Development* (London: Routledge, 1997), 67, "For much of known human history, population and total output tended to grow at about the same rate, so that per capita income remained roughly constant." Although he argues for an earlier date, economist William Easterly claims that the conventional date for the emergence of the concept of development economics is President Harry Truman's inaugural address of 1949:

> We must embark on a bold new program for making the benefits of our scientific advances and industrial progress available for the improvement and growth of underdeveloped areas ... More than half the people of the world are living in conditions approaching misery ... For the first time in history, humanity possesses the knowledge and the skill to relieve the suffering of those people.

William Easterly, *The Tyranny of Experts* (New York: Basic Books, 2012), 43. For an account of the evolution of "modern growth theory," see Robert J. Barro and Xavier Sala-i-Martin, *Economic Growth* (New York: McGraw-Hill, 1995), 9–13.

of the industrialized world, and that background dominated their approach to the rest of the world.

THE EMERGENCE OF NEO-INSTITUTIONAL ECONOMICS

Most prominent in economists' minds were two contemporaneous episodes of rapid economic growth: the forced march industrialization of Stalin's USSR and the Marshall Plan. Both were interpreted as accelerated capital accumulation stimulated by direct state intervention.[2] Stalin transferred forced savings from the rural sector to industry; the Marshall Plan transferred capital and technology from the United States to postwar Europe. Western economists also had their own countries' histories, which all included the transformation from agrarian societies to industrial ones. Why should the new developing countries be any different? Further impetus for simplicity came from the nature of economics as an academic discipline that prized elegance, certainty, and universality, not detail, ambiguity, and difference. If the variety of the emerging nations demanded attention, it could be left to the anthropologists. Meanwhile the economists would discover, distill, and diffuse the universal imperatives for development, whatever the peculiarities of any specific country.

Out of this intellectual world emerged modernization theory, which dominated American foreign aid policy into the 1980s. Most prominent and closely identified with the Kennedy and Johnson administrations of the 1960s was Walter W. Rostow's stages-of-growth model of development, which combined a linear conception of development with faith in a mechanical connection between capital investment and growth. Rostow argued that all nations able to mobilize an adequate level of savings and investment would proceed through the same developmental stages that had characterized the economic history of Europe and North America: from a traditional subsistence economy, through "take-off" and rapid growth, culminating in a society characterized by mass consumption.[3] Strong state intervention was necessary to create the

[2] Not all economists interpret the Marshall Plan as primarily about capital. See Deepak Lal, *Poverty and Progress: Realities and Myths about Global Poverty* (Washington, DC: Cato Institute, 2013), 170: "The [Marshall Plan] did not work as some present-day aid advocates contend. It was not the finance that was vital; rather, the support for institutions, the credibility it gave to reforms, and the movement towards democracy allowed Europe to live in peace after being the major theater of two world wars."

[3] Rostow's five stages were traditional society, preconditions to take-off, take-off, drive to maturity, and mass consumption. See Chantal Thomas, "Re-Reading Weber in Law and Development: A Critical Intellectual History of 'Good Governance' Reform." http://scholarship.law.cornell.edu/lsrp_papers, 65–78. The story of the transformation of development economics and economists from the 1950s through to the 1990s is acerbically and concisely told in chapter eight

preconditions for take-off and to guide the economy, but if the state managed domestic and international markets, rather than denying them, Rostow and other leading development economists of the day, including W. Arthur Lewis, Raul Prebisch, and Albert Hirschman, agreed that every economy would eventually catch up with the developed world.

The pace of convergence would be determined by the amount of investment and the application of an economic formula known as the Harrod-Domar growth model,[4] which stipulated a direct economic relationship between capital stock and growth. The more a country could invest, the faster it would move from stage to stage. The prescription was stunningly simple once the preconditions had been created: increase aggregate capital stock or, in layperson's terms, add money. If a poor country could raise its investment rate through either domestic savings or international transfers and use it to create productive capital stock, growth at a corresponding level would follow.

The combination of Rostow and Harrod-Domar was hugely attractive. It was simple, universal, ahistorical, and optimistic. All countries start from the same condition, that of a traditional society. They are not products of colonialism or international manipulation, nor are they constrained by geography or culture. One need not worry about the quality of their courts or whether they had clear property rights. One could deal with them simply as a new set of societies at the predevelopment stage from which all societies began. If they complied with the stages-of-growth formula, all they needed to climb the ladder of convergence was capital. Since all economies would respond to the same policies in the same way, the only thing that kept these societies from success was the "investment gap," which could be addressed by political will, and indeed this prescription justified the transfer of significant amounts of financial and technical assistance from rich to poor countries.

Alas, it did not work. By the 1980s there was a perception that the billions transferred to poor countries had been largely wasted. Elites, personified by thoroughly unattractive dictators, had become rich, but consistent and widespread growth had not occurred. Furthermore, by 1980 the intellectual and political environment in the West had changed. The political consensus exemplified by European democratic socialism and Kennedy and Johnson had been replaced by Ronald Reagan and Margaret Thatcher, and Rostow and welfare economics had been supplanted by Milton Friedman and the University of Chicago school of economics. It was time for change, and the

---

of Dani Rodrik's *The Globalization Paradox: Democracy and the Future of the World Economy* (New York: Norton, 2012).

[4] For an entertaining, if not exhaustive, explanation, see Komilla Chadha, *Harrod-Domar Model in 7 mins*. www.youtube.com/watch?v=2wYpiWk_WTQ, 2013.

top-down, state-centered, capital-dependent model of Rostow and Harrod-Domar was replaced by the bottom-up, market-centered *laissez faire* globalization of the Washington Consensus.

What did not change was the confidence of (a different group of) Western economists and policymakers that they had the answer to world poverty. Equally optimistic, universal, and simple, the Washington Consensus recoiled from the restructure-society, manage-markets, add-money prescription and advocated less government intervention and more reliance on unfettered markets. "Add money" became "hands off" and neo-classical economic liberalism became the recipe for economic growth everywhere. While modernization theory may seem simple in hindsight, the Washington Consensus was even more so and, importantly, a lot cheaper. The rich no longer had to transfer capital to the poor; they just had to help poor states install a neo liberal-market economy and open their economies to trade and investment. Once these conditions were met, comparative advantage would allocate valuable assets to their most productive users across the globe, and growth would follow.

By the 1990s, however, confidence in simple answers had begun to wane. Spectacular failures like the "big bang" privatization advice offered to and embraced by Russia coupled with the now impossible-to-ignore success of China had muddied the intellectual waters, and the rhetoric, if not the practice, of "one size fits all" had become unfashionable. While development economics had not quite gone anthropological, there was a general rejection of the universality of both approaches and an acceptance that poor countries differed from rich ones and from each other in ways that were important to the work of international aid organizations.

Unfortunately, many of those differences in history, geography, culture, for example, were difficult to address, and others, like politics, were beyond the bounds of legitimate intervention. What was available was the reform of the institutions by which poor countries were governed and, by the turn of the twenty-first century, the dominant approach had become the neo-institutional economics of Ronald Coase,[5] Harold Demsetz,[6] and Douglass North,[7] which forms the theoretical basis for the existing emphasis on law and

5 Ronald H. Coase, "The Problem of Social Cost," *Journal of Law & Economics* 3 (1960): 1.

6 Harold Demsetz, "Toward a Theory of Property Rights," *American Economic Review* 57 (1967): 347.

7 Douglass C. North, *Structure and Change in Economic History* (New York: Norton, 1981) and *Institutions, Institutional Change and Economic Performance* (Cambridge: Cambridge University Press, 1990). Mancur Olson is another economist associated with institutional economics. See Mancur Olson Jr., "Big Bills Left on the Sidewalk: Why Some Nations Are Rich, and Others Poor," *Journal of Economic Perspectives* 10 (1996): 3, 22.

property rights. As we shall see in the next section, however, the relevance of legal institutions to economic growth had been noted decades earlier.

Max Weber and Economy and Society

The fundamental idea driving global legal reform today – that law is a necessary, if not sufficient, precondition to economic growth – originated in Max Weber's *Economy and Society*,[8] written almost a century ago. Weber was a legally trained German sociologist intent on explaining why capitalism emerged in Europe and nowhere else. To do so, he used historical methods to isolate what was distinctive about European society, which required not only knowledge of Europe but also of the great civilizations that did not develop capitalism, most notably India, Islam, and China.

In *The Protestant Ethic and the Spirit of Capitalism*, Weber identified two unique features of European society that facilitated capitalism: its religion and its law. We will return to Weber's sociology of religion briefly, but for now suffice it to say that he claimed that the divine value accorded to work, entrepreneurism, and the accumulation of wealth by northern European religion inspired the populace to work for spiritual fulfilment and personal worth as well as for material gain. Our focus, however, is on his identification of the legal systems of continental Europe and specifically the theories of nineteenth-century German legal science as fundamental to the emergence of capitalism.

Weber emphasized that it was the nature and structure of legal institutions, not the content of the rules, that created capitalism. Four features were central: legal institutions were autonomous from political administration and religious dogma; law was a body of man-made rules, not traditional or divine norms; adjudication was determined by preexisting general rules rather than ad hoc facts; and rules were applied universally to all members of the polity. European law was distinctive on all these dimensions and therefore more "logically formally rational," by which he meant internally consistent and independent of outside influences, whether religious beliefs, cultural values, or policy goals.

Because European law succeeded in insulating legal decisions from such factors, Weber concluded, it created a society dominated by an autonomous rule system that provided the predictability necessary for capitalism to flourish. Rules were obeyed because they were accepted as legitimate and they

[8] Published in German as *Wirtschaft und Gesellschaft*, English translation edited by Guenther Roth and Claus Wittich, *Economy and Society* (Berkeley: UC Press, 1978). For a comprehensive account of Weber's contribution, see David M. Trubek, "Max Weber on Law and the Rise of Capitalism," http://digitalcommons.law.yale.edu/fss_papers/4001?utm_source=digitalcommons.law.yale.edu%2Ffss_papers%2F4001&utm_medium=PDF&utm_campaign=PDFCoverPages.

were legitimate because they were created rationally, not because they were divine or magical. Formal legal institutions were equally legitimate, partly because they too were rational but also because the rules were created, interpreted, and applied openly and according to stable procedures that were distinct from and independent of other sources of social control such as religion and politics. The result was a highly calculable lawyer's utopia where people could know their rights and duties, could predict when legal coercion would be employed, and could be confident that no other source of social control would constrain any behavior allowed by law. To put these ideas in the vocabulary of postwar development economics, once property rights were assigned and contracts enforced, arm's length transactions became possible, and one of Rostow's preconditions for take-off had been met. When combined with the divine imprimatur to make money, the market took care of the rest, and European capitalism was born.

Or so goes the cartoon version of Weber's sociology of law. When we look more closely, three issues complicate the direct applicability of his work to development today. First is his broad definition of law. As was true for his successors Demsetz and North, law was any "order ... externally guaranteed by the probability that physical or psychological coercion will be applied by a staff of people in order to bring about compliance or avenge violation." What is missing here from the perspective of a conventional definition of property rights is the state. Conversely, what has been added is the possibility of coercion and persuasion as enforcement techniques. A religious order, a Girl Scout troop, a weekend soccer league, or any other organization with a differentiated *staff* could have law as long as it could mobilize the common will and resources to *avenge* violations. Equally importantly, Weber did not claim that Europe was unique in having law; all of the great civilizations had law. Thus, it was neither the presence of a legal order in itself, nor the location of that order in the state that produced capitalism, but a specific formal normative order, potentially differentiated from state and society, that produced development.

The second limiting issue is the specificity of the question that animated his work. Weber was explaining a single historical event: the role of law in the emergence of European capitalism. He was not predicting what would happen if German legal science and judicial institutions were transplanted elsewhere. Unfortunately, as we shall see later in this chapter, part of the attraction of property theory to development economics is precisely its technical, noncontingent nature, not unlike the mechanical nature of the Harrod-Domar formula or the theory of comparative advantage. Once the calculability of Weberian law and its causal power in producing economic growth are linked to a unique set of religious beliefs and historical conditions, its utility is greatly diminished. After all, while it may be relatively easy to computerize Kampala's courts or enact a Ugandan version of the Japanese Civil Code, it is harder to engender a belief in Calvinist predestination in the average Ugandan fishing on Lake Victoria. It is much easier simply to assume that what worked in one place will work in the next – or to ignore the origins of Weber's ideas entirely.

A third and even less well-remembered part of Weber's legacy is his normative view of a formal legal order. The rule of law is now a universally revered ideal.[9] Virtually everyone from American politicians applauding or condemning a county clerk's refusal to obey a judicial order on religious grounds to the Fourth Plenum of the Chinese Communist Party advocates the rule of law for every political and social ill. Weber had a different view, perhaps because he specified a particular legal order rather than leaving it to be defined as the good in whatever form or context it appeared. Weberian legalism helped beget capitalism and capitalism had unquestionable social benefits, specifically the relatively productive allocation of resources, but Weber did not equate efficiency to fairness or logically formal legal rationality to justice. His views were more nuanced:

> Formal justice guarantees the maximum freedom for the interested parties to represent their formal legal interests. But because of the unequal distribution of economic power, which the system of formal justice legalizes, this very freedom must time and again produce consequences which are contrary to religious ethics or political expediency.[10]

He specifically called property into question: "[T]he principle of formal legal equality" provides "the propertied classes the factual 'autonomy'" that legitimizes the domination of workers by capitalists. In other words, once we realize that legalism, while seeming to constrain the state, actually strengthens it and that formal legal equality masks substantive inequality and injustice, Weber's characterization of the rule of law becomes not quite so bright and shiny.

Neo-Institutional Economics: Coase, Demsetz, and North

Weber's insights about the role of law in development have their contemporary home in neo-institutional economics and the ideas of Ronald Coase, Harold Demsetz, and Douglass North. Summarizing these ideas is dangerous, but most accounts would begin in 1960 when Coase, in his article *The Problem of*

[9] One commentator observed that the "apparent unanimity in support of the rule of law is a feat unparalleled in history." Brian Tamanaha, *On the Rule of Law: History, Politics, Theory* (Cambridge: Cambridge University Press, 2004), 3.

[10] Weber, *Economy and Society* 2, 812.

Social Cost, introduced the economic concept of externalities into legal discourse and linked them to property and contract rights. He argued that a central function of the government in a market economy was to assign property rights and enforce contracts so that individuals could bargain among themselves to internalize externalities and thereby maximize net social welfare. Coase himself stressed repeatedly that exchange would produce these results only in an imaginary transaction costs-free world, but his warnings, like those of Weber, have been lost in the rush for simple answers to complex problems. In today's world, Coasian bargaining stands for the assumption that owners will use contracts to exchange property rights until they enjoy all the benefits and bear all the costs of the use of their property.

Absolutely essential are property rights, and it was Demsetz's *Toward a Theory of Property Rights* that integrated Coase's insights into the discourse of rights. Demsetz used an anthropological account of the response of the Montagne Indians of Labrador to the rising value of beaver pelts to argue for the superiority of individual over communal property.[11] Before the arrival of the French and the commercialization of the beaver trade in the seventeenth century, the Montagne had used their hunting ground communally – all members of the group could hunt anywhere and without limit. Because the demand for beaver was low and their number high, the effect of each hunter's take was *de minimus*. Once the French started to buy beaver pelts, however, demand increased and over-hunting began to have a palpable impact on the interests of the group as a whole. Communal ownership provided no means to address either the fair distribution of the cash proceeds from common lands or the problem of a declining beaver population. The solution was a shift to individual hunting grounds and the consequent internalization of the cost of hunting to each individual owner.

The Montagne story is classic fodder for American law school students and excerpts are included in many first-year property textbooks to introduce the idea that property rights have economic consequences and are adjustable instruments for engendering economic growth. Indeed, Demsetz is the "go-to" theorist when legal reformers need theoretical backing for what they assume is the universal common-sense value of formal, judicially secured property rights.

[11] Demsetz describes the shift as privatization, stating that before the commercialization of the beaver trade, "there did not exist anything resembling private ownership in land." Demsetz, "Toward," 352. I prefer to characterize this shift as individual rather than private because I question whether the Montagne considered their communal hunting ground to be open to all other groups. In other words, I suspect that they considered the land in question to belong to their group; it was thus private, rather than public. It is also worth noting that the holder of the right after privatization or individualization was likely the family, not a sole individual.

Unfortunately, three elements of his theory are often overlooked in the process of moving from theory to action in poor countries. Each is fundamental.

To begin with, Demsetz conditioned the benefits of property rights and Coasian bargaining on five conditions:

1. All property rights must be assigned.
2. The cost of policing property rights must be zero.
3. The cost of exchanging property rights must be zero.
4. All owners of property rights must be utility maximizers.
5. Change in the distribution of wealth cannot affect demand patterns.[12]

The problem with these conditions as a guide to policy is not that they are rarely all met simultaneously. It is the stark reality that *none* of them is *ever* satisfied. Transaction costs inevitably plague the protection and exchanging of assets; the demand curves of the wealthy, the middle class, and the poor differ; and no one is a utility maximizer if one defines utility to mean maximizing quantifiable gain. (Of course, if one defines utility broadly enough, everyone becomes a utility maximizer because it means simply that one does what one does.) Identifying things to which property rights have not been assigned is more difficult, but that is because we have difficulty recognizing valuable assets such as social trust, parental care, or a full moon free of advertising as potentially subject to property rules. Normative and technological change, however, can make the unimaginable commonplace – granting Social Security credit to stay-at-home parenting or an Apple logo on the face of the moon – but for Demsetz's theory to operate, such new property rights must have been anticipated by and incorporated into the property system. Of course, to point out the impossibility of the realization of a transaction cost-free world does not mean that Demsetz's theory cannot be an enormously fruitful guide to policy. It means simply that one must be fully and constantly aware that his world, like Coase's, is an imaginary one and very different from the "second-best" world in which we operate.

The next forgotten aspect of his theory is definitional. As he famously explained:

> Property rights are an instrument of society and derive their significance from the fact that they help a man form those expectations which he can reasonably hold in his dealings with others. These expectations find expression in the laws, customs, and mores of a society.[13]

[12] Harold Demsetz, "Some Aspects of Property Rights," *Journal of Law & Economics* 9 (1966): 61, 62.

[13] Demsetz, "Toward," 347.

For Demsetz, therefore, property organizes social behavior by enabling individuals to know what they can and cannot do in relation with other members of society. As with Weber, the constraints on action are expressed by social practice and values as well as formal law. Once a person understands a specific constraint, she can abide by its limitations or, if the right is formal and hence transferable, buy the power to ignore it. Conversely, when another's act harms a person, the "laws, customs, and mores" of society will determine whether she has the power, informally or through litigation, to prevent the harm or must either suffer the injury or pay the actor to desist.

It is clear that Demsetz envisaged formal law as one means of defining and enforcing property rights, but it is equally clear that contemplation of formal legal institutions did not play a central role in his work. In *Toward a Theory of Property Rights*, he rarely refers to the legal process and mentions "court" only once in the phrase "the state, the courts, or the leaders of the community," reinforcing the interpretation that for him formal law is only one means of social action. Thus, influential residents in an affluent neighborhood may have no legal right to exclude, for example, an AIDS hospice, affordable housing, or other locally undesirable land use (LULU), but politics, customs, mores, and simply the transaction costs facing the proponents of the LULU may prevent it as effectively and predictably as a zoning regulation. It is not, in other words, the formal law that explains the fact that such uses are rarely located in such neighborhoods. In a more commercial context, members of a trade association may have no formal legal power to enforce price cartels, but various forms of retaliation and pressure may effectively prevent industry members from violating unwritten or even illegal agreements.[14] According to Demsetz's broad definition, however, all such constraints on action, if consistent and stable enough, qualify as property rights, even though in the cartel example complying with and enforcing the right constitutes criminal behavior.

The last limitation on the relevance of Demsetz's work for guiding legal reform is that his description of the process of creating, modifying, and exchanging property rights is equally broad, or perhaps it is more accurate to say that it is nonexistent. He never mentions, for example, *how* the Montagne decided to individualize their hunting grounds. For him – and for many other economists – it is as if more efficient property rights simply appear, as if the reallocation of social entitlements is an organic, almost natural process: "property rights arise when it becomes economic for those affected by externalities

[14] For an account of the enforcement of one such "property right," in this instance the power of a criminal gasoline import cartel to prevent cheating by a rogue member, see Frank K. Upham, "The Man Who Would Import: A Cautionary Tale about Bucking the System in Japan," *Journal of Japanese Studies* 17:2 (1991): 323.

to internalize benefits and costs."[15] At other times, he seems to give property rights a will of their own: "The property rights system began to change."[16] Or he avoids agency altogether: "These adjustments have arisen in Western societies largely as a result of gradual changes in social mores and in common-law precedents."[17] The mechanism by which general changes in a population's "customs and mores" constrain individual behavior or by which a state's judiciary is persuaded to change the law is left to the imagination of the reader.

A key constant, not only with Demsetz but also with contemporary advocates of legal reform, is the absence of conflict. There are winners but no losers. On the societal level, any clash of interests remains offstage. On the individual level, change in the allocation of rights and hence in economic wealth is brought about by voluntary exchanges or, more accurately, no coerced change is necessary because the satisfaction of the five contra-factual assumptions means that there are no transaction costs to frustrate bargaining. Every exchange makes every party better off than prior to the exchange. Although the law may change, nothing as nasty as the destruction of property rights ever occurs.

Demsetz was fully aware of the imaginary nature of this world. Following his colleague Coase, he expressly lamented that the discipline of economics was disastrously distorting his ideas:

> The view that now pervades much public policy economics implicitly presents the relevant choice as between an ideal norm and an existing 'imperfect' institutional arrangement. This *nirvana* approach differs considerably from a *comparative institution* approach in which the relevant choice is between alternative real institutional arrangements. [Italics in original][18]

Unfortunately, the warnings of both Demsetz and Coase have been largely ignored by international law reformers. The tendency to assume away reality has, if anything, accelerated, and economists' concentration on the theoretical potential of property rights to the neglect of the conflict inherent in their formation, modification, and exchange may bear some of the blame, but the most prominent neo-institutional economist, Douglass North, did not make the same mistake.

Unlike Coase and Demsetz, North stresses the contingent nature of property rights. He agrees that the market exchange of property rights will determine

[15] Demsetz, "Toward," 354.
[16] Ibid. 352.
[17] Ibid. 350.
[18] Harold Demsetz, "Information and Efficiency: Another Viewpoint," *Journal of Law and Economics* 12:1 (1969), 1.

whether a society grows, stagnates, or declines, but he is under no illusion that efficient property rights spontaneously "arise," "change," "emerge," or "adjust" on their own. On the contrary, he warns us that "it is the polity that defines and enforces property rights" and that there is an "inherent tendency of political-economic units to produce inefficient property rights."[19] Efficient property rights are rare because the state will produce property rights that will favor the powerful within the political-economic units that constitute the polity. If the constellation of those units is such that efficient property systems are created, we are in a Panglossian best of all possible worlds, but as North notes, history has only occasionally produced such arrangements and the sustained economic growth that they enable. More common are property structures that favor elite interests over social welfare.

Central to the creation and enforcement of efficient property rights and hence determinative of economic performance are what North calls institutions, which, echoing Weber and Demsetz, he describes as "made up of formal rules, informal norms and the enforcement characteristics of both."[20] Among the constituent parts of institutions, it is the informal norms, which he has called "mental models" and "ideologies," that are most important:

> While the formal rules can be changed overnight, the informal norms change only gradually. Since it is the [informal] norms that provide the essential 'legitimacy' to any set of formal rules, revolutionary change is never as revolutionary as its supporters desire, and performance will be different than anticipated.[21]

North thus not only shares the broad definition of property rights of his predecessors but also ties Demsetz's "customs and mores" to political legitimacy, without which courts in developing countries will not be able to enforce even, or perhaps especially, the most efficient property rights structures that foreign experts can devise.

[19] North summed up the relationship between the state and property rights in 1990: "It is exceptional to find economic markets that approximate the conditions necessary for efficiency. It is impossible to find political markets that do. Because it is the polity that defines and enforces property rights, it is not surprising that efficient economies are exceptional." "The New Institutional Economics and Third World Development," in *The New Institutional Economics and Third World Development*, ed. J. Harris et al. (London: Routledge, 1995), 17–27 at 20. North is not alone among scholars in recognizing the contingency of efficient institutions including property rights. See, e.g., David Kennedy, "Some Caution About Property Rights as a Recipe for Economic Development," *Accounting, Economics, and Law* 1 (2011): 1.

[20] North, "The New Institutional Economics," 26.

[21] Ibid. For a general discussion, see Douglass North, *Structure and Change*, 45–58.

Before we turn to how international actors have implemented the ideas of neo-institutional economics, let's review what it has to say about property rights. First, they are complex social structures that depend on North's ideologies and mental models and Demsetz's customs and mores as much as or more than on the statutes, court decisions, and regulations of the formal legal system. Second, although both Coase and Demsetz are frequently evoked for property rights' ability to achieve efficiency by the internalization of costs and benefits, the full realization of that ideal is entirely hypothetical. The best that market transactions can achieve in practice is the least flawed of an array of inefficient options – what Demsetz termed the comparative institution approach rather than a search for nirvana.

Third, formal legal regimes are not inherently socially beneficial, much less efficient. On the contrary, North explains why they are more likely to serve the interests of the few than those of the society at large, and Demsetz reminds us that even when we achieve a set of beneficial property rights, we may soon have to change them. Although we often hear of the importance of "secure property rights" to development, securing inefficient or obsolete property rights will benefit only those whose interests they serve and will prevent necessary adjustment.

Fourth, although the poverty of developing countries implies that their property institutions are not optimal, change is unlikely to be easy or quick. While property *law* can be "changed overnight," the creation of beneficial property institutions in Demsetz's and North's broader sense requires time for the underlying mental models to change. Even when a regime has the resources and will to introduce the best-practices model of a particular legal form, therefore, implementation will be as dependent on bottom-up acceptance as on top-down expertise and innovation. Finally, although the need to shift from less to more efficient property structures is a constant refrain in the literature, the process is always depicted as bloodless. New rights appear, but the old ones, and the interests of their owners, are not destroyed. In a word, in neo-institutional economics, there are winners, but no losers. In real life, there are both.

PROPERTY THEORY IN PRACTICE: THE LAW AND DEVELOPMENT MOVEMENTS

We now turn from economic theory about law to the policies that international aid organizations have adopted in practice to reform poor countries' legal systems in what have become known as the first and second law and development movements. As we shall see, legal reform has been relegated from being an end in itself to being a means of achieving market efficiency. What has remained consistent has been the rejection of the complexity and caution of the founders of neo-institutional economics in a search for formulaic answers. Indeed, the current faith in the efficacy of formal law is more reminiscent of the linear progress of Walter Rostow or the Harrod-Domar investment gap than it is to the economic history of Douglass North.

Law and Development without Economics

In the 1960s, at the height of capital fundamentalism, the stages of growth, and the Cold War, public and private elites in the United States undertook to "modernize" the legal systems of the newly independent countries of the developing world, not solely for purposes of growth, but also "to protect individual freedom, expand citizen participation in decision-making, enhance social equality, and increase the capacity of all citizens rationally to control events and shape social life."[22] Just as now, the legal systems of the developing world were seen as wanting, not because they didn't secure property rights and enforce contracts, but because they didn't provide the citizenry with the tools to participate in the strong state that could structure society and prepare it for take-off. The target was not simply correcting a technical failure (the lack of formal land titles or inefficient courts, for example) it was cultural transformation. The legal systems of the global South were seen as "inflexible and unresponsive to policy demands. Thus, it was believed that by exporting the antiformalist, policy-oriented approach to law associated with American liberal legalism, state officials would be given the tools to reorient economic systems in a way that could spur modernization."[23]

Then and now, two assumptions sustained this effort: that Western legal institutions were portable and that transporting them was desirable. In that fundamental sense little has changed, but because the aim was to change legal culture rather than correct technical failings, the place to start was legal education. Seen as doctrinal and formalistic, Third World law faculties were to be converted to the "pragmatic problem solving" and "policy-sensitive" approach assumed to characterize American legal education. A description of one set of such efforts will illustrate the spirit of the movement and the depth of the desired transformation:

[22] David M. Trubek and Marc Galanter, "Scholars in Self-Estrangement: Some Reflections on the Crisis in Law and Development Studies in the United States," *Wisconsin Law Review* (1974): 1062.

[23] Scott Cummings and Louise G. Trubek, "Globalizing Public Interest Law," *UCLA Journal of International Law & Foreign Affairs* 13 (2009): 1, 10.

> Programs aimed at achieving legal education reform were funded by agencies of the U.S. government and U.S. foundations throughout the 1960's. SAILER (Staffing of African Institutions For Legal Education and Research), begun in 1962 with support from the Ford Foundation, sought to improve African legal education by exporting American law graduates to African universities for the purposes of teaching and aiding in research. The program gained subsequent additional financial support from both the Rockefeller Foundation and the Peace Corps. CEPED (Center For Study and Research in Legal Education), started in 1966 with funding from AID and the Ford Foundation, contemplated reform of Brazilian legal education. The Center was established to teach Brazilian lawyers with the use of such U.S. teaching techniques as the "Socratic" discussion of cases, texts and legislative materials, the problem method, and study of the social sciences. The developers of CEPED hoped not only to give young Brazilian lawyers an understanding of new developmental legislation, but also to eventually affect the Brazilian law schools by creating both materials to be used in their curricula and a new breed of law teachers to utilize those materials.[24]

It is worth repeating the goal of these philanthropic and governmental efforts: the re-making of Third World legal systems in the American image. Legal education was the entry point, but only the initial step in building a new American-style legal system. Like their economist colleagues, practitioners of the first law and development movement knew little about Latin American or African legal systems but they did know their own, or at least an idealized vision of it. The economists had the Marshall Plan and Stalin's forced march to industrialization; the lawyers had *Brown* v. *The Board*, the civil rights legislation of the 1960s, and the criminal procedural reforms epitomized by *Miranda*. Capital accumulation and investment had seemingly done the trick for Europe and the Soviet Union and a cadre of dedicated lawyers had changed invidious rules and transformed American society; it was time to take that transformation to the rest of the world. US Supreme Court Justice William O. Douglas captured the spirit of the age:

> These newly developing nations need our help – not only our money and machines and food, but also the great capital of knowledge accumulated by our professors ... Refrigerators and radios can be easily exported – but not the democratic system. Ideas of liberty and freedom travel fast and far and are contagious. Yet their adaptation to particular societies requires trained people, disciplined people, dedicated people. It requires lawyers.[25]

[24] Trubek and Galanter, "Scholars," 1066.

[25] Ibid. Trubek and Galanter, "Scholars," 1067–8, footnote 16. American lawyers' missionary zeal for proselytizing has deep roots. For its centuries-long history with China in particular,

It did not matter whether these lawyers knew anything about the particular society they were transforming. After all, if dedicated lawyers could end segregation in Arkansas, how much harder could it be to create democracy in the Democratic Republic of Congo?

The answer, of course, was "very," and the results were deeply disappointing to practitioners, as eloquently described by two founders of the movement, David Trubek and Marc Galanter:

> They have come to see that legal change may have little or no effect on social economic conditions in Third World societies and, conversely, that many legal "reforms" can deepen inequality, curb participation, restrict individual freedom, and hamper efforts to increase material well-being.[26]

The most obvious lesson learned was the naïve ethnocentrism of advocates and practitioners, but it was not the only one. The Ford Foundation/USAID model of development put great faith in the social and political potency of courts and litigation. They had just witnessed, after all, the courts' substantial role in changing the course of American race relations and police practices. What they discovered, however, was that courts and law are not universally powerful, indeed are often irrelevant, and, even more troubling, not always benign. They discovered, in other words, what Max Weber had said long before and Douglass North was saying around the same time: that law is all too likely to serve the interests of the few and powerful, that law can be, in a word, bad.

Profound disillusionment followed. As Trubek and Galanter summarized it: "Law and development scholars [and practitioners] know that they can no longer automatically accept the inherent moral worthiness of either assistance or scholarship, but they lack clear guidelines to distinguish between what is worthy and what is not." The first law and development movement was dead. Faith in the potency of rich countries' law, however, was not. It was just napping.

Development Economics Discovers Law

The second law and development movement, also known as the rule of law movement, did not spring from the enthusiasm of Justice Douglas or the philanthropy of the Ford Foundation. Nor is it an attempt to change the legal

---

see Jedidiah J. Kroncke, *The Futility of Law and Development: China and the Dangers of Exporting American Law* (Oxford: Oxford University Press, 2016).

[26] Trubek and Galanter, "Scholars," 1080.

cultures of the Third World. On the contrary, it was born in the office of the General Counsel of the World Bank and is aimed primarily at implementing the technical fixes necessary for poor countries' legal systems to support market transactions and thereby propel those countries out of poverty. There is more to it, of course. Just as the lawyer idealists of the 1960s had assumed economic growth would follow political liberalization, the economists of the 1990s assumed that the democratic virtues of the rule of law would accompany the wealth created by market-friendly law reforms. But it was no longer a lawyers' game. They still played, but they played by economists' rules and for economists' ends. When it came to the role of law in attaining those goals, furthermore, the "pragmatic problem solving" and "policy-sensitive" judiciary was replaced by formalism and technical proficiency.

Our current, almost ecstatic faith in formal law has its apotheosis in the vision and charisma of one man, Hernando de Soto, whom we will meet briefly in the next section of this chapter, but it started with that most mundane of documents, a legal memo, in this instance World Bank General Counsel Ibrahim F. I. Shihata's 1990 *Legal Memorandum on Issues of "Governance."*[27] By the late 1980s the Bank's role in the global economy had expanded from being a source of foreign exchange for specific development projects to a level of involvement in the structure and management of developing countries' economies that threatened to violate the prohibition of political activity in the Bank's Articles of Agreement.[28] Shihata's task was to bring these arguably political initiatives within the ambit of permitted economic activities. His solution was to link economic performance to governance and good governance with the "rule of law" and to distinguish both from politics. He defined law as a non-ideological "system based on abstract *rules* which are actually applied and on functioning *institutions* which ensure the appropriate application of

[27] Available at Ibrahim F. I. Shihata, *The World Bank Legal Papers* (New York: Springer, 2000), 245–82.

[28] Article IV, Section 10: Political Activity Prohibited

> The Bank and its officers shall not interfere in the political affairs of any member; nor shall they be influenced in their decisions by the political character of the member or members concerned. Only economic considerations shall be relevant to their decisions, and these considerations shall be weighed impartially in order to achieve the purposes stated in Article I.

Three particular issues arose in the 1980s that threatened to violate Section 10: efforts to improve governance in African countries, the creation of the European Bank for Reconstruction and Development intended to help Eastern European countries' economic and political transformation, and the increase in "adjustment lending" premised on changes in borrowing countries' government structures.

such rules." [Italics in original.] For Shihata such a system was necessary to development:

> Reform cannot be effective in the absence of a system which translates them into workable rules and makes sure they are complied with. Such a system assumes that: a) there is a set of rules which are known in advance, b) such rules are actually in force, c) mechanisms exist to ensure the proper application of the rules and to allow for departure from them as needed according to established procedures, d) conflicts in the application of the rules can be resolved through binding decisions of an independent judicial or arbitral body and e) there are known procedures for amending the rules when they no longer serve their purpose.[29]

Shihata went on to state that, without the rule of law, the fates of both individuals and enterprises will be left "to the whims of the ruling individual or clique" and that only predictable rules and due process can provide the "general social discipline" that makes economic growth possible.

The attraction of uniform rules impartially applied is universal. It is certainty closer to the lay vision of law than the policy-driven vision of the 1960s, but it has an academic pedigree as well. Antonin Scalia, once a law professor, then a Supreme Court justice, argued in *The Rule of Law as a Law of Rules* that clear rules consistently and objectively applied is not only the best way to manage children's television watching but also the best way to govern the allocation of resources within a complex society. It is not surprising therefore that by 1996 the World Bank had fully adopted Shihata's rhetoric, with particular reference to property rights:

> Property rights are at the heart of the incentive structure of market economies. They determine who bears risk and who gains or loses from transactions. In so doing they spur worthwhile investment, encourage careful monitoring and supervision, promote work effort, and create a constituency for enforceable contract. In short, fully specified property rights reward effort and good judgment, thereby assisting economic growth and wealth creation.[30]

Conversely, without enforceable property rights, investment will not occur because investors will not be able to protect their assets from private theft and state expropriation. With Shihata's characterization of law as nonpolitical, the cartoon version of Weber and the nirvana world of Demsetz were freed to become the theoretical basis for the world's leading developmental institution.

29 Shihata, *Legal Papers*, 273.
30 World Bank, *From Plan to Market: World Development Report* (1996), 48–9.

Consistent with these beliefs, the past quarter century has seen the return of externally initiated and financed legal reform projects in poor countries, but this time directed at creating market-friendly legal rules and enhancing the judiciary's role in their enforcement. The faith in *laissez faire* private ordering is as breathtaking as it was at the height of the Washington Consensus, but now conditioned on the correct legal system. In the words of the chief counsel of the World Bank's Legal and Judicial Reform Practice Group,

> [A]llocative efficiency will be ensured once clear property rights are established and guaranteed by the government, and that the government does not need to intervene further, because once private parties have clearly defined property rights, they can bargain for an efficient outcome. A free and robust market can thrive only in a political system where individual freedoms and property rights are accorded respect and where redress for violations of such rights can be found in fair and equitable courts.[31]

While no one has quite called for "formalism" or "rigidity," the quest for ad hoc problem solving by policy-oriented judiciaries conversant in the social sciences is over. Doctrine, once disdained as the stultifying core of Third World legal education, is no longer pejorative, at least when expressed as Scalia's "law of rules" and focused on property and contract.

Although Amartya Sen's call for attention to a range of human "capabilities" and "functionings" to complement the quantitative metrics of economic growth has led to a broader conception of development generally,[32] there has been no analogous call for flexible pragmatism or local sensitivity on the legal side. On the contrary, two movements emphasizing the virtues of certainty and precision have accelerated the drive for formality initiated by Shihata's memo. The first has been the campaign to title and register informally held land inspired by de Soto's claim that formal ownership will give the poor access to needed credit, which we will examine in Chapter 6 when we discuss the reform of Cambodia's land law. Now we turn to a different dimension of the quest for certainty, the desire to know *precisely* where on a quantitative spectrum of development readiness each developing country sits and *exactly* which aspects of its legal system need to improve for it to grow. The path to such knowledge is paved by indicators, lists ranking countries from first to 189th on a range of characteristics from the time necessary to get a building permit to the degree of transparency, competitiveness, or corruption.

[31] Maria Dakolias, "A Strategy for Judicial Reform: The Experience in Latin America," *Virginia Journal of International Law* 36 (1995–6): 167, 168.

[32] Amartya Sen, *Development as Freedom* (New York: Alfred A. Knopf, 1999).

Indicators and the Search for Certainty and Precision

The magic of indicators is the conversion of highly contested concepts such as property rights or rule of law into a single number. Once each country's legal system has been given a number, ranking follows automatically, and policy-makers within development agencies can confidently evaluate and compare poor countries on dozens of indices of development readiness.[33] Even more magical, they can do so without going to the countries, doing background reading on their societies and economies, or even consulting experts with first-hand knowledge. The International Property Rights Index (IPRI) can illustrate.

The IPRI is published annually by the Property Rights Alliance (PRA), a Washington-based advocacy group "dedicated to the protection of property rights all around the world."[34] The index evaluates and ranks 129 countries on the security of their property rights. The PRA does no original or independent research into the conditions of any of these countries, instead relying on publicly-available data from ten indices produced by other entities, chiefly the World Bank and the World Economic Forum. Since these indices are themselves the products of surveys, usually of people designated as experts in one or more facets of each country's legal system, the IPRI is a survey of surveys of surveys. The PRA does not create the questions and cannot ensure consistency in the use or meaning across surveys of even the most basic of terms such as "property," "rights," or "law."

Other indicators, created by all sorts of organizations, from politically engaged groups like the PRA to international bodies like the UN and the World Bank, vary wildly, but almost all share a fundamental characteristic: They skip the research aspect of knowledge production and rely solely on the aggregation of subjective opinion data. As a result, they can say virtually nothing about how any given country's legal system operates. Knowing, for example, that Cameroon is ranked 111th on the IPRI and Burkina Faso 101st is unlikely to help anyone navigate either country's legal system, but if the task is to decide which nation is worthy of preferential access to developed country

33 The number of covered countries varies. The World Bank's *Doing Business*, probably the most influential indicator, covers 189 countries. The International Property Rights Index, <internationalpropertyrightsindex.org>, produced by the Property Rights Alliance, covers 129, and the Rule of law Index, produced by the World Justice Project, <http://worldjusticeproject.org/>, covers 102. For a comprehensive review and analysis of the phenomenon, see Kevin E. Davis, Angelina Fisher, Benedict Kingsbury, and Sally Engel Merry, eds., *Governance by Indicators: Global Power through Quantification and Rankings* (Oxford: Oxford University Press, 2012).

34 International Property Rights Index 2015 <https://s3.amazonaws.com/ipri2015/IPRI+FINAL+110415.pdf>

markets, concessionary loans, or development assistance, that ten-country gap can be determinative. After all, should a mid-level World Bank or USAID official choose Burkina Faso for a loan and the loan not be repaid, she can always explain that Burkina Faso was ranked ten places higher than Cameroon. Her rationale is objective, clear, and conclusive – even if, in substantive terms, it is nonsensical.

This scenario is not implausible. As one group of critics put it in 2012, "the burgeoning production and use of indicators in global governance has the potential to alter the forms, the exercise, and perhaps even the distributions of power in certain spheres of global governance."[35] This may actually understate the case. The World Bank has described the purposes of their own *World Development Indicators 2015* (WDI) as follows:

> [It] provides a compilation of relevant, highquality [*sic*], and internationally comparable statistics about global development and the fight against poverty. It is intended to help policymakers, students, analysts, professors, program managers, and citizens find and use data related to all aspects of development, including those that help monitor progress toward the World Bank Group's two goals of ending poverty and promoting shared prosperity.[36]

This statement is worth unpacking. The WDI provides policymakers, analysts, program managers, and social actors with statistics that will lead to data that can guide them in fighting poverty. The statistics, however, reflect only the subjective opinions of a tiny number of Bank-selected "experts" about questions that Bank employees believe should guide decisions by policymakers in their reshaping of poor societies. This data is then ordinally ranked so that it can be internationally comparable: Burkina Faso was 3.0 of 6.0 in 2014, Cameroon 2.5.[37] With this data the Bank project manager, the local government bureaucrat, or foreign legal reformer is ready to take action: to draft a new land law, to approve a large-scale lease to an agri-business, or to grant tariff preferences for agricultural products.

Indicators have become an intrinsic part of the process by which the rich world monitors and influences the remaking of poor countries' legal systems including their property law. What is troubling, of course, is that indicators by their very nature may exacerbate the tendency to abstract, simplify, and generalize complicated and particularistic phenomena that we have already

35 Davis et al., *Governance by Indicators*, 4.
36 http://issuu.com/world.bank.publications/docs/9781464804403
37 http://data.worldbank.org/indicator/IQ.CPA.PROP.XQ

seen is endemic in the implementation of development theory. As Davis et al., put it:

> Indicators are typically aimed at policymakers and are intended to be convenient, easy to understand, and easy to use. Yet, the transformation of particularistic knowledge into numerical representations strips meaning and context from the phenomenon. In this numerical form, such knowledge carries a distinctive authority that shifts configurations and uses of power and of counter-power. This transformation reflects, but also contributes to, changes in decision-making structures and processes.[38]

Fetishizing Property Rights, Ignoring Reality

Despite these flaws, government, as James Scott pointed out in *Seeing Like a State*, cannot proceed without simplification. If one's mandate is to govern the world, it would be foolhardy to dismiss outright a device that simplifies the complex reality of 189 countries. Similarly, when working to improve the quality of developing countries' legal systems, it would be foolish, even cynical, to reject an ideal with the allure of "the rule of law, not of men" or "secure property rights." It is important, therefore, not to caricature reform efforts as I claim practitioners have caricatured neo-institutional economics. Indeed, the World Bank is not unaware of the dangers inherent in the undifferentiated transplantation of Western models, and as we shall see in Chapter 6, elements within the Bank, if not the development world more generally, have learned that administrative efficiency and normative appeal should not preclude analysis and sensitivity to context.

It is unfortunately true, however, that any recognition of the dangers of radical simplification and the automatic application of undefined Western ideals to poor countries will inevitably encounter the reality of both the demands of global governance and economists' (and others') natural desire for simplicity, elegance, and certainty, traits that Friedrich Hayek called "physics envy."[39] It is not surprising, therefore, that as one World Bank researcher ruefully concluded, the "message" of the need for caution and the eschewing of simple

[38] Davis et al., 6. See Chantal Thomas, "Re-Reading Weber," http://scholarship.law.cornell.edu/lsrp_papers, 80–5, for an account of the scholarly attempts to build complexity into law and development practice.

[39] *The Counter-Revolution of Science* (Indianapolis: Liberty Press, 1952/1979).

answers "does not seem to have been clearly communicated to policy analysts and decision makers, with negative consequences."[40]

The almost inevitable result on the ground is an approach to development that mistakes ideology for reality. The search for precision substitutes ordinal lists for local knowledge, and the need for clear and secure property rights ignores history. As we shall see in the next two chapters, in the course of their development England, the United States, and Japan all destroyed the very kind of formal property rights the rich world is now forcefully urging on the rest of the world. And it is not only ancient history that is ignored. The last 35 years of Chinese growth without best-practices property rights or anything approaching the rule of law have had virtually no impact on theory or practice.

The point is not that the seamless transplantation of the computerized title systems of the West to Cambodia would be a bad thing – on the contrary. Nor is it that the West is being hypocritical. The substitution of ideology for reality has much more important consequences. To ask a poor country to create a politics-free, rule-fetishizing judiciary to enforce legally defined and created property rights is unwise not only because it asks developing countries to do the impossible, but also because it ignores what has engendered rapid economic growth throughout history, i.e., the "rationalization" – that is, the destruction – of existing property rights and their transfer from less to more productive sectors of society. To provide context, we now turn to two successful, if painful, instances of that process, the exclusion of English villagers from the commons and the transformation of American water law.

40 Klaus Deininger, *Land Policies for Growth and Poverty Reduction: A World Bank Policy Research Report* (World Bank Report # 26384), xvii. http://documents.worldbank.org/curated/en/485171468309336484/Land-policies-for-growth-and-poverty-reduction

3

Property and Markets

England and America

In this chapter we examine two case studies of the destruction of property rights in response to market opportunities. The first chronicles three centuries of the English enclosure movement and the incremental elimination of villagers' rights to enter and forage on their lord's land. The second uses an American water law case, *Sanderson and Wife* v. *Pennsylvania Coal Co.*, to illustrate the nineteenth-century transformation of American property law to accommodate commercialization and industrialization. Both accounts emphasize two aspects of these complicated phenomena, the nature of the interests lost and the role of formal legal institutions in the process of social restructuring. There is no attempt to create a model or derive best practices of market adjustment, but the lessons from these unique events can be applied to seemingly unrelated social phenomena of today. Indeed, the subsequent chapters on the transformation of Japanese, Chinese, and Cambodian property law and social structure will draw heavily on the analysis of what happened centuries earlier on distant continents.

WHEN SHEEP ATE MEN: THE ENGLISH ENCLOSURE MOVEMENT

In 1550, 80 percent of the English population was engaged in agriculture; only 20 percent of those farmers produced for the market; and productivity was so low that the English population had stagnated at six million for centuries. Three centuries later, 80 percent of the population worked off the land, those that farmed were overwhelmingly "businessmen farming for the market," and the population was approaching 20 million.[1] The most striking aspect of England's agricultural revolution for us, however, is not these statistics, or even the fundamental

[1] See www.urbanrim.org.uk/population.htm for the history of England's population in graphic form. See generally John Hatcher, *Plague, Population and the English Economy, 1348–1530* (London: Macmillan, 1977) and E. A. Wrigley and R. S. Schofield, *The Population History of England 1541–1871* (Cambridge, UK: Cambridge University Press, 1989).

change in the nature of land ownership that drove them. It is the political and legal process that facilitated the dispossession of an entire class without the widespread violence and disruption that usually accompanies such change.

At the beginning of the sixteenth century, even though the lord of a manor may have owned a parcel of land in a sense approximating our notion of legal title, other village residents, the commoners, had rights to use that land in specific ways that severely limited the lord's power over the land. The result was an agricultural topography that was dramatically different from that of today. Although enclosed fields called "closes" existed that resembled contemporary agricultural patterns, they were the exception and relatively small:

> [T]here were much larger fields, perhaps up to several hundred acres in extent, subdivided into long strips of land forming the units of land ownership. Sometimes these strips were separated by a grass strip but often there was no obvious physical boundary between the strips. Fields were often ploughed in a pattern of ridges and furrows to assist drainage, and each strip could correspond to a single ridge or furrow. Strips were often grouped together into units called furlongs or lands, but a subdivided field might also have little closes within its boundaries.[2]

The differences did not end with the physical layout. Commoners had a bewildering array of property rights beyond the right to cultivate their strips, including: the pasturage of "commonable animals" (ponies, cattle, donkeys, mules) and sheep; mast (foraging by pigs); turbary (cutting of peat); marl (digging of clay); and estover (gathering of firewood). All of this applied not only to cultivated land but also to wetlands, mountain areas, and other non-arable "wastes," and all of it had to be honored by the owner. By 1850, in contrast, property ownership had become essentially identical to forms common in today's developed world. A single owner had exclusive control of unified land. That owner could grant a variety of rights to others – leases, easements, *profits à prendre* (the right to take things from the land, hence covering turbary, marl, estover, etc.), and numerous types of servitudes – but the decision was individually controlled, and any departure from unified and exclusive possession of the land flowed from that choice.

The underlying force that led to these changes was the market, first the rising price of wool in the fifteenth and sixteenth centuries that made it profitable for owners to shift from communal cultivation to exclusive sheep pasturage, and later rising grain prices that made mono-cropping even more profitable than wool production. In this sense, the enclosure movement is

[2] Mark Overton, *Agricultural Revolution in England: the Transformation of the Rural Economy, 1500–1830* (Cambridge, UK: Cambridge University Press, 1987), 23.

no more interesting than any other market adjustment, like American textile manufacturers moving production from New England to the American south and then overseas. What made the enclosure movement iconic is that it necessitated the elimination of the commoners' myriad property rights to the land, which in turn led to the restructuring of the preexisting way of life.

English landownership has always been unequal, but even the minimal rights held by commoners gave them substantial economic sustenance, social standing, and legal power over their lives. By the nineteenth century, however, ownership was not only extremely concentrated but also free of any inherent obligations to neighbors or residents. The majority of the population had not only lost their means of livelihood but also whatever status and influence their ancestors had enjoyed. Entire villages were depopulated and a new class of landless poor was created, which many observers argue provided the demographic foundation for the industrial revolution.

The process was long, varied, and regionally fragmented, and the legal and political contexts were in constant flux. In addition, the historiography is vast and contested[3] and what follows cannot provide a comprehensive account of the process or resolve the myriad ideological debates, but as distant and arcane as the conditions of sixteenth-century English agriculture may seem to those interested in, say, communal grazing rights in contemporary East Africa, the elimination of a set of property entitlements developed for one social structure and the simultaneous creation of a legal framework to meet new economic, political, and technological demands is functionally identical.

This account will therefore highlight two aspects of the English enclosures that are directly relevant to developing countries today, and to all countries where rapid economic growth is occurring or desired. The first is the nature and range of property rights destroyed, what the commoners lost and the lords gained. The second is the varied and contradictory roles of formal legal institutions, initially the King's Bench and later the Parliament: in other words, the

[3] Two seminal discussions of the enclosures in England are those of Karl Marx in *Capital, Volume II* and Barrington Moore, Jr., *The Social Origins of Dictatorship and Democracy: Lord and Peasant in the Making of the Modern World* (New York: Beacon, 1967). Other historians have examined documents and archives for evidence of the negative effects of enclosure and commercialized agriculture upon the lower agrarian classes. Important studies of this type are R. H. Tawney, *The Agrarian Problem of the Sixteenth Century* (London: Longman, Green and Co., 1912) and J. L. Hammond, *The Village Labourer, 1760–1832* (London: Longman, Green and Co., 1918), both relying on careful attention to first-hand records, in contrast to the former authors' reliance on secondary accounts. These works look at the two great waves of enclosure in England. Tawney examines the sixteenth century when arable land was transformed to sheep pasture. Hammond looks at the enclosures of the late eighteenth and early nineteenth centuries, often referred to as the Parliamentary Enclosures because they occurred through a process of public and private parliamentary legislation.

"how" as opposed to the "what" of property rights destruction. This account, like any overview of a complex social process, must be selective, but can provide historical and comparative context to the analysis of contemporary problems.

The Legal Framework

Although widespread enclosures did not occur until the rise in the international price of wool in the sixteenth century, the legal framework dated to the Statute of Merton of 1235, which allowed the lords of manors for the first time to exclude villagers from the use of the lords' "wastes, woods, and pasture."[4] The lords were constrained, however, by the requirement that they demonstrate to the justices of the assize that the enclosure left sufficient common pasture for the freeholders, inferior landowners on the manor whose tenure was not derivative of the feudal power of the lord. Village residents below the freeholders, a bewildering and evolving variety of commoners (villeins, serfs, freemen, and more), had diminishing rights depending on whether they possessed either land or a house and had hence been inscribed on the manor rolls as "copyholders." Where an individual fit in the hierarchy largely determined whether he and his family were totally dispossessed and became agricultural laborers or could evolve into yeoman farmers and perhaps prosperous tenants on a large estate.

For our purposes, what matters is that from the beginning enclosure entailed intricate legal and class distinctions. At the top of the commoners were the freeholders; next were the copyholders; and at the bottom were the serfs, later freemen, who lived in rented cottages and who were thus not inscribed as copyholders. What all these groups shared was a determination to resist the destruction of entitlements dating from time immemorial on which their way of life depended. The resistance took many forms, including sporadic instances of violence that are strikingly similar to the "mass protests" of contemporary Chinese farmers and that are characteristic of rapid economic growth anywhere. What English commoners of the sixteenth century had that twenty-first-century Chinese and Cambodian farmers often do not enjoy, however, was a realistic chance to challenge their dispossession in court, and even the lowliest of the group initially had some success.

[4] See generally George Shaw-Lefevre, *English Commons and Forests: The Story of the Battle During the Last Thirty Years for Public Rights over the Commons and Forests of England and Wales* (London: Cassell and Company, 1894).

This ended, however, in 1603 with *Gateward's Case*. The residents of the village of Stixwold, in Lincolnshire, cited an ancient custom to justify their right to pasture cattle in defiance of the lord's enclosure of the waste. With reasoning that would be familiar today, the King's Bench unanimously declared that they lacked standing, as recounted in a disapproving nineteenth-century account:

> The judges ... assigned the pedantic and technical reasons that the inhabitants of a district are too vague a body to enjoy a right of a profitable nature; that such a right can only attach to property; and that, if conceded, there would be no person or persons in a position to extinguish or release the right.[5]

The point is that the judges did not make the politically charged declaration that the plaintiffs did not have a preexisting right to use the waste, but simply the narrow legal determination that they did not have the legal personality necessary to vindicate whatever rights they may have in court.

Their reasoning exemplifies the ability of law to lower transaction costs by effectively disabling existing property rights. If village-wide customary usage had been protected judicially, collective action problems might well have prevented the manor waste from ever entering commerce, no matter how socially valuable commercialization might have been. In other words, although the court was not going to deny explicitly the villagers' rights to use the common, it certainly was not going to allow them to prevent a productive response to the opportunity presented by the rise in international wool prices.

Gateward's set the standard, but as the same nineteenth-century account put it, "As often happens ... when the judges have laid down a broad proposition of a questionable character, their successors endeavor to whittle it down, or to set it aside by some ingenious quibble."[6] So, in subsequent cases, the King's Bench held that formal incorporation could give villagers the legal personhood necessary to defend their property rights. In other cases, where the evidence of long-standing use was particularly strong, judges relied on the tried and true legal fiction of a "lost grant." Once long-term use of the lord's manor was shown, the court would presume that the commoners must have had a right to use it. Otherwise how could one explain the lord's acquiescence?

[5] Lefevre, *English Commons*, 14–5. The *Gateward's Case* is discussed in Andrea C. Loux, "Persistence of the Ancient Regime: Custom Utility and the Common Law in the Nineteenth Century," *Cornell Law Review* 79 (1993): 183 and E. P. Thompson, *Customs in Common: Studies in Traditional Popular Culture* (New York: The New Press, 1993), 134–7. For a twenty-first-century iteration of functionally identical reasoning, see the 2012 US Supreme Court case *Golan* v. *Holder*, 565 US 1, where the court held that "the public" has no property right when things of value are removed from the public domain.

[6] Lefevre, *English Commons*, 15.

Such persistent, widespread use without permission of another's land was only understandable if there had been at some point a royal charter, now forgotten by all, granting such a right. But in the vast number of cases, the *Gateward's* doctrine held, and, once the lords had satisfied the Statute of Merton's requirement of sufficient pasturage for the freeholders or reached an agreement with them to share the profit of the enclosure, they were able to proceed without any consideration of the preexisting rights of the rest of the commoners.

The Contingency of Law

The end result of the enclosures was the transformation of English agriculture from a level barely able to meet the nutritional requirements of the farmers themselves to a fully commercial sector that not only produced for international and domestic markets but also provided the economic and demographic foundation for eighteenth- and nineteenth-century industrialization. What made this vast increase in human wealth possible was the dispossession of the lowest and most numerous ranks of rural society. Without the rights to cultivation, forage, and pasture that had sustained their ancestors for centuries, they either became agricultural laborers or joined the new industrial proletariat. But focusing solely on what was lost would miss an equally important lesson: that this "revolution of the rich against the poor"[7] was based not on lawless violence or brutal oppression but on the careful manipulation of the law. The process did not weaken the regime, as it may be doing in rural China today; it legitimized it, as a brief review of the process in two contrasting nineteenth-century cases can demonstrate.

The first is the successful resistance to the enclosure of Wimbledon Common. Wimbledon Manor dates from an eleventh-century grant from Edward the Confessor to the See of Canterbury, and for the next eight centuries it went back and forth among the crown, the church, and various earls, dukes, duchesses, marquises, and other members of the elite. During this time, at least one owner tried to enclose the manor, but it was not until the nineteenth century that Lord Spencer made a determined attempt. The villagers, through the Commons Committee, resisted, and excerpts from a contemporaneous account can give a sense of the gravamen of the conflict:

> The Rolls of the Manor date from the time of Edward IV … [and] are replete with interesting facts, bearing on the condition of the Manor and the rights of its freehold and copyhold tenants. Besides the Rolls, there is a record of the Customs of the Lordship of Wimbledon, taken from the Black Book of

7 Karl Polanyi, *The Great Transformation* (New York: Rineholt, 1957), 35.

> Canterbury… and also a Parliamentary survey of the Manor made in 1649. The earlier Court Rolls abound with orders and regulations respecting the rights of cutting wood and furze … During the summer the wood was not allowed to be taken; but it was usual for the Parish Beadle to go round every year at Michaelmas with his bell, and "cry the Common open." He went round again at Lady Day to "cry it shut."[8]

In 1864, when Lord Spencer began the parliamentary enclosure process, he claimed that enclosure would benefit all and tried to buy out the commoners. They rejected his offer and stalemate followed:

> It may be taken as certain that Lord Spencer … was disappointed by the action of the Commoners; he did not recognise their right to interfere with him in the mode in which he proposed to deal with the land. They, on their part, contended that their rights were such as to place them at least on a par with the lord, and to make their consent necessary to any dealings with the waste in the public interest. They complained that the action of Lord Spencer's steward was such as to ignore and set aside their rights, and if permitted to continue, would have destroyed their claim to a voice in the destiny of the Common.[9]

The Commoners Committee filed suit in 1866 asking for a declaration of their rights and an injunction against the Lord's violation thereof. When the parties' respective research into the history of the common tended to favor the commoners and the likelihood that the court would find a lost grant, the Lord agreed in 1870 to relinquish all rights to the common in return for a fixed annual payment equal to the average of what he had derived from the common over the previous ten years.

The Wimbledon case can represent the many instances over the three centuries of enclosures when village inhabitants were able to use the law to protect their property rights, but it is important to remember that in most cases, the lord prevailed and enclosure proceeded. The Wimbledon commoners won, not only because they could prove long-established use, but also because they had the resources to fight: there were many able lawyers living around the commons and one particularly rich man living on the commons was willing to fund the battle.

The contemporaneous case of the common of the Manor of Tollard Farnham is more typical and a direct descendant of *Gateward's*. Unlike *Wimbledon*, *Tollard Farnham* began not with proactive litigation by the

[8] Ibid. 92–3.
[9] Ibid. 95.

inhabitants but as a defense to trespass actions brought by Lord Rivers against three villagers for cutting and carrying away furze in a forest deer preserve. In contrast to Wimbledon Common, Tollard Farnham was purely rural and lacked lawyers or affluent residents, but the defendants received assistance from the Commons Society, a nineteenth-century organization trying to preserve common lands, and were therefore able to do the historical research that had carried the day in *Wimbledon*. The arbitrator assigned to find the facts for the Court of Exchequer found, "That from the commencement of legal memory, down to the date of the inclosure [*sic*], there had been 'user' on the Common by a very large number of persons in the cutting of furze and hazel wood for fuel [which user] was exercised continuously, openly, and of right."[10]

The Court of Exchequer noted the evidence of sustained use, but nonetheless drew on *Gateward's* to decide that the lack of some form of village incorporation would mean an indefinite number of potential individual beneficiaries of the right and "necessarily lead to the destruction of the subject-matter of the Common."[11] As a result, the court refused to entertain the legal fiction of a lost grant and gave Lord Rivers the victory and "whatever satisfaction was to be derived from wresting from the laboring people of one of his many parishes an user and custom which had undoubtedly existed from time immemorial … the last vestige of a sense of property in the land on which they were born and bred."[12]

The Enclosures as Social Change

As the contrasting results in *Wimbledon* and *Tollard Farnham* indicate, cases presenting very similar facts could come to very different results, but the point is not which judges were legally correct or what the doctrine should have been. The point is that the commoners' loss of property rights became legal cases at all. The enclosure movement was not a Demsetzian "adjustment" among a small and homogeneous ethnic group trying to reap windfall benefits that would dwarf the losses of individual families. Enclosure was an existential struggle played out among classes with directly conflicting interests, one that a leading historian of the movement characterized as "agrarian warfare" and analogous to what is happening now to Cambodian and other subsistence farmers in poor countries, although with the important difference that globalization has added international agribusiness to the list of players.[13]

[10] Ibid. 219.
[11] Ibid. 220.
[12] Ibid. 222.
[13] Tawney, *Agrarian Problem*, 237.

Perhaps no one has described the stakes better – or more melodramatically – than Sir Thomas More in the sixteenth century, recounting an imaginary conversation with a "Cardinal":

> [Y]our sheep that were wont to be so meek and tame, and so small eaters, now, as I heard say, be become so great devourers and so wild, that they eat up, and swallow down the very men themselves. They consume, destroy, and devour whole fields, houses, and cities.[14]

Nor was the process seen as a morally neutral market adjustment, as perhaps our hypothetical textile factory's relocation might have been seen in twentieth-century New England. To More, it was class warfare and greed was its driver:

> [N]oble men, and gentlemen, yea and certain Abbots, holy men no doubt, not contenting themselves with the yearly revenues and profits, that were wont to grow to their forefathers ..., nor being content that they live in rest and pleasure nothing profiting, yea much [injuring] the weal public, leave no ground for tillage: they enclose all into pastures, they throw down houses, they pluck down towns, and leave nothing standing.[15]

And the human toll could be stunning:

> [T]hose good holy men turn all dwelling places and glebeland into desolation and wilderness. Therefore that one covetous and unsatiable cormorant and very plague of his native country may ... inclose many thousand acres ... within one pale or hedge, the husbandmen be thrust out of their own, either by [collusion] and fraud, or by violent oppression they be put besides it, or by wrongs and injuries they be so wearied, that they be compelled to sell all: by one means therefore or by other, either by hook or crook they must needs depart away, poor, silly, wretched souls, men, women, husbands, wives, fatherless children, widows, woful mothers, with their young babes ... Away they trudge, I say, out of their known and accustomed houses, finding no place to rest in.[16]

More exaggerates and simplifies. The three centuries of enclosure were much more complex, the morality more ambiguous, and the consequences less universally dire than he would have his sixteenth-century readers believe.

[14] Pasturage destroying Husbandry in *Utopia Book I* from Henry Craik, ed. English Prose 1916 Vol. I Fourteenth to Sixteenth Century online at Bartleby.com.

[15] Pasturage destroying Husbandry in *Utopia Book I* (1516) from Henry Craik, ed. English Prose 1916 Vol. I Fourteenth to Sixteenth Century online at Bartleby.com.

[16] Pasturage destroying Husbandry in *Utopia Book I* from Henry Craik, ed. English Prose 1916 Vol. I, Fourteenth to Sixteenth Century found online at Bartleby.com

Most important, however, few would advocate a return to subsistence agriculture for England or anywhere else, and it was not solely a material gain. Perhaps the two most compelling and contrasting discussions of the enclosures – those of Karl Marx in *Kapital, Volume II* and Barrington Moore in *The Origins of Dictatorship and Democracy* – agree that the process marked the beginning of modernity. Both see the enclosures as fundamental to the formation of market capitalism and modern society, but draw contrasting lessons therefrom. Marx focuses on the enclosures as a movement that took historic rights away from the least powerful members of feudal agrarian society and transformed villagers into an agrarian and urban proletariat. Moore looks at the flip side of this capitalist development, arguing that the liberation of peasants from feudal tenures and the gradual nature of the process contributed to the creation of democracy in England.

Both are correct in that the enclosures were a prerequisite to capitalism, dramatic increases in material wellbeing, and political modernization. Although Marx and Sir Thomas More may overstate the coercive nature of enclosures, they are correct that the rural poor lost the property rights that were the foundation of their way of life and often received in return little more than the magic of legal process. But Barrington Moore is also correct to say that it was the sense of justice inherent in even a flawed legal process that enabled English society to eat its cake and have it too: to retain its sense of the sanctity of property while enjoying the rapid economic growth made possible by the destruction of the property rights of its weakest members. And while class warfare is not usually conducted via litigation, the English enclosures were not, as we will see, an aberration.

WHEN POLLUTION WAS *NATURAL*: THE TRANSFORMATION OF NINETEENTH-CENTURY AMERICAN PROPERTY LAW

At the start of the eighteenth century, the United States had an agrarian, subsistence economy, with little commercial activity beyond a small number of coastal towns and a legal system that protected local interests and values. By the end of the century, the American economy had changed, and so had its law. Common-law rules that had threatened to slow or halt commerce and industry had been weakened or eliminated, and citizens who had previously been able to protect themselves from various forms of harm arising from growth had to adjust. Judges, not legislators, played the central role in the doctrinal change, thus allowing the rising capitalist class to avoid the direct and open conflict with vested interests that the democratic process would have required. As we have seen, the idea that judges would play a role in social change is not new, but their role in nineteenth-century America went beyond merely reacting to it, beyond the delaying and legitimating, the calming of conflict with the balm of legal process as in *Gateward's* and *Wimbledon*, to the active facilitating of social change.[17]

As with the enclosures, the process was complex and the historiography is contested. Although no one has resorted to the hyperbole of Sir Thomas More's man-eating sheep, some scholars, most notably Morton Horwitz, have characterized the courts' role as class warfare that exacerbated economic inequality by substantially reducing legal liability for harm caused to others across a wide range of doctrines. Others, like William Nelson, have argued that the process is better understood as a contest between established agrarian interests and emerging industrial entrepreneurs pursuing the opportunities provided by changing technology.[18] Fortunately for our purposes, there is general agreement that judges reallocated property rights in the same market-enabling direction of the enclosures. In doing so, they not only eliminated legal barriers to economic growth but also recognized and articulated a fundamental shift in American legal and social structure. As Nelson put it, property and specifically landed wealth was no longer the political and moral "keystone of a well-ordered community [that] had to be secured so that liberty could

[17] I have drawn heavily on two sources: Morton J. Horwitz, *The Transformation of American Law, 1780–1860* (Cambridge: Harvard University Press, 1977) and William E. Nelson, *The Americanization of the Common Law* (Athens: University of Georgia Press, 1994 edition). As one would expect of a Marxist perspective on American legal history, Horwitz's interpretation has drawn criticism. Note Gary T. Schwartz's reviews at "Tort Law and the Economy in 19th Century America: A Reinterpretation," *Yale Law Journal* 90 (1981): 1717, and Gary T. Schwartz, "The Character of Early American Tort Law," *UCLA Law Review* (1981): 641. See also Stephen F. Williams,"The Book Review," *UCLA Law Review* 25 (1977–1978): 1187. Schwartz and Williams dispute the class-based aspects of Horwitz's analysis and conclusions, but Horwitz's and Nelson's characterization of the changes in riparian law, which is the focus of this section, is largely accepted. For example, Williams in his otherwise highly critical review of Horwitz states, "It seems generally agreed that in the nineteenth century riparian water law in the eastern United States evolved from a concept of 'natural flow' to one of 'reasonable use'." Williams, "Book Review," 1197. Note that in his use of "evolved" Williams, like Demsetz and other economists noted in Chapter 2, elides the human political action required to change the law.

[18] If anything, Nelson's evaluation of the nineteenth-century transformation of American law is even more fundamental than Horwitz's. For Nelson, it goes beyond "the judiciary's willingness to sacrifice ancient property rules to the promotion of economic development" to a "new theory of property" where American courts "in effect ... no longer view landed wealth as a legally protected source of individual security but as a commodity whose prices in the market depended on its productivity." For Nelson, it was not solely the favoring of one class over another but also and more importantly a social and legal "shift from a set of essentially religious, other worldly values to a set of materialistic, worldly values." Nelson, *Americanization*, 163–4.

continue to exist [but] merely one of several commodities in the marketplace" to be manipulated to serve the needs of commerce and growth.[19] To get a concrete sense of how that process unfolded, we turn to one instance of this struggle between agrarian property rights and industrialization.

The Sanderson Cases[20]

In 1868, J. Gardner Sanderson and his wife, Eliza McBrair Sanderson, purchased a plot of land along Meadow Brook, a spring-fed stream of "perfectly pure" water, in the city of Scranton, Pennsylvania. Over the next two years, the couple completed construction of a home on their property and built a dam to supply a fish and ice pond, an irrigation system, a fountain, and a cistern.

Meanwhile, by 1870, the Pennsylvania Coal Company had sunk a mine two miles upstream from the Sandersons' home, which, as all coal mines in the area did, filled with acidic groundwater. The company pumped the water into Meadow Brook, which rendered the stream "worse than worthless." The fish died. The willows withered. The cistern corroded. By 1873, the water was unfit for domestic use. The Sandersons had to get water from other sources.

The Sandersons brought suit in the Court of Common Pleas of Luzerne County. Since Pennsylvania followed the water law doctrine of natural flow, which prohibited any use that would interfere with the quality, quantity, or impetus of water flow, they were likely confident of victory. Unfortunately for them, however, they drew Judge William H. Stanton, whom, according to the *New York Times* of March 5, 1879, "nobody respected or trusted" and who indeed was unsympathetic to their plight despite what appeared to be clear law in their favor. Stanton peremptorily dismissed their action on the grounds of *damnum absque injuria* (loss without injury). Stanton did not deny that the Sandersons were injured but ruled that discharging water is a necessary incident to mining and that Scranton was coal mining country. The Sandersons appealed.

[19] Nelson, *Americanization*, 163.

[20] The summary of facts given here comes from the four Pennsylvania Supreme Court decisions in *Pennsylvania Coal Co.* v. *Sanderson and Wife*: 86 Pa. 401 (1878) (hereinafter *Sanderson I*), 94 Pa. 302 (1880) (*Sanderson II*), 102 Pa. 370 (1883) (*Sanderson III*), and 113 Pa. 126 (1886) (*Sanderson IV*). I have selected the *Sanderson* line of cases because they illustrate the judicial and political roles clearly, indeed one might say melodramatically, not because the Pennsylvania Supreme Court was the first or most influential court to change the law. The transition from natural flow to reasonable use is more conventionally attributed to Justice Joseph Story in the 1827 *Tyler* v. *Wilkinson*, 24 F. Cas. at 474. See discussion at Horwitz, *Transformation*, 38. Note that although Mrs. Sanderson was the owner of the property, "Sanderson and Wife" in the caption of the case was necessitated by the doctrine of coverture, which gave the husband legal control of his wife's property during the marriage.

At the Pennsylvania Supreme Court, the coal company challenged the court to make explicit what Judge Stanton had left implicit and adopt the cause of one of the state's dominant industries: "The law must be adjusted to our great industrial interests." The court stuck with the doctrine, however, and, in a decision that came to be known as *Sanderson I*, found for the Sandersons by a vote of six to one. In an opinion written by Justice Warren Woodward, the court held that the interests of coal did not trump the well-settled law of the state, certainly not to the extent of depriving agricultural interests of a vital property right, and applied the principal *sic utere tuo ut alienum non lædas* (use your own as to not injure another's) to reverse Stanton and find the coal company liable. The court did not deny the defendant's economic contribution to the community, but noted that "however laudable an industry may be, its managers are still subject to the rule that their property cannot be so used as to inflict injury on the property of their neighbors." The case then returned to the Court of Common Pleas, where a jury found for the Sandersons and awarded damages in the amount of $250. Neither party was satisfied, and both separately filed writs of error, setting the stage for *Sanderson II* and *III*.

Having previously failed in its policy-based attack on the natural flow doctrine itself, the coal company took a less direct approach and assigned for error the lower court's refusal to allow the defendant to show that it was the custom of Lackawanna County to dispose of mine water in this manner and to rule that such custom, if proved, was a full defense to the pollution. Although framed as custom, the company was ironically employing the same argument used by commoners in *Wimbledon* and other enclosure cases under the fiction of a lost grant: that long-established use of another's property without permission would trigger an irrebuttable presumption that the user had received at some point in the past the legal right to use the property in that manner.

The *Sanderson II* court didn't buy it. In an 1880 opinion written by Justice Isaac Gordon, the court echoed Justice Woodward's acknowledgement in *Sanderson I* that industrial companies contribute to the "general good" but pointed out that "they are, however, not the less instituted and conducted for private gain, and are used and enjoyed as private rights over which the public has no control." Gordon then rejected Penn Coal's custom argument on both factual and legal grounds. On the facts, he noted that the defendant's mine was the first mine on Meadow Brook and had existed no longer than the plaintiffs' home and therefore that any "custom" lacked both generality and longevity. On the law, he concluded that even if the mine had established a long-standing practice, "a custom, such as this, would not only be unreasonable but also unlawful, and therefore worthless."

The Supreme Court was not finished with the case, however, because the Sandersons had separately appealed, and here is where they and the agricultural interests they represented snatched total defeat from the jaws of partial victory. Had they been satisfied with the measure of damages in *Sanderson I*, the case would have ended with the vindication of their right to enjoy the Meadow Brook in its natural state. A legal win and modest damages, furthermore, might have been a compromise that would have upheld existing doctrine, partially compensated the victims, but allowed mining to continue. From a twenty-first-century law and economics perspective, it might even have represented the best of all Coasian worlds: the judicial internalization of negative externalities.

For the Sandersons, however, the $250 damage award did not come close to the injury to their land or their property rights, and they appealed and assigned for error the trial judge's jury instructions that had permitted the jury to reduce their damages because they had been receiving water from a city source for at least five years. The Supreme Court in *Sanderson III* agreed and, in 1883, returned the case to the Court of Common Pleas for retrial with more liberal damages instructions. Two years later a jury awarded the Sandersons $2,872.74. The defendant then took its second writ of error in the case, and the Pennsylvania Supreme Court got its fourth bite at the apple.

THE REASONING OF *SANDERSON IV*

As the first substantive paragraph of the court's opinion made clear, the fourth time was the charm for the Pennsylvania Coal Company. After bizarrely claiming that "the main question involved is one of new impression in this state,"[21] Justice Silas M. Clark starkly stated the court's and society's dilemma:

> It has been stated that 30,000,000 of tons of anthracite and 70,000,000 of bituminous coal are annually produced in Pennsylvania. It is therefore a question of vast importance, and cannot, on that account be too carefully considered; for, if damages may from time to time be recovered, either in the present form or as for a nuisance, punitive sums may be resorted to prevent repetition, or to compel the abatement of the nuisance. Indeed, if the right to damages in such cases is admitted, equity may, and under the decisions of this court undoubtedly would, at the suit of any riparian owner, take jurisdiction, and upon the ground of a continuous and irreparable injury, enjoin the operation of the mine altogether. Whatever rights Mrs. Sanderson may have to the use of this water, and whatever remedy she may have in this case, or

[21] *Sanderson IV*.

> in any other form, in law or in equity, is the right and remedy of every other riparian owner along Meadow brook [*sic*]; and whatever may be the rights and remedies of the owners on Meadow brook are, of course, the rights and remedies of all other riparian owners throughout the Commonwealth.

So much for Coasian bargaining. The increase in damages by over 1,000 percent had already drawn into question any possibility that the coal industry could afford to compensate downstream riparian owners seriatim, but the real issue all along had been potential plaintiffs' right to injunctive as well as monetary relief. Riparian rights are property rights and a land owner who can prove violation of his right to the natural flow of a stream or river can in principle obtain an injunction regardless of the relative social value of the offending behavior. Once the court acknowledged that any victim of water pollution could shut down any polluting coal mine, the choice was clear: enforce agriculture's property rights or destroy them and allow industrial growth. Late in his opinion, Justice Clark states the court's choice openly if harshly:

> The plaintiff's grievance is for a mere personal inconvenience; and we are of opinion that mere private personal inconveniences, arising in this way and under such circumstances, must yield to the necessities of a great public industry, which although in the hands of a private corporation, subserves great public interest. To encourage the development of the great natural resources of a country trifling inconveniences to particular persons must sometimes give way to the necessities of a great community.

Pennsylvania's choice may have been inevitable. Virtually every other modern nation has made the same choice for the simple but rarely acknowledged reason that industrialization at costs acceptable for developing countries is impossible without violating the economic entitlements of the preexisting agricultural regime. In a rule-of-law country like the United States, those entitlements will be embedded in formal property rights such as the natural flow doctrine. Changing property rights, however, is not easy – indeed that is the whole point of property rights – so what is of interest to us is not the choice but the means to that choice and here is where the genius of *Sanderson IV* lies. It successfully transferred important property rights and the wealth that they produced from one social class to another, and it did so without violence and without de-legitimatizing either Pennsylvania's political process or its legal system. For that reason, it is worthwhile looking further into Clark's opinion. For although it was his sentence above that captured the motivation for the decision, it is his reasoning that demonstrates an important judicial role in economic growth.

The Sandersons had a legal right to the *natural* flow of the Meadow Brook. To allow coal mining and industrialization to continue, therefore,

Pennsylvania had either to change property law explicitly through legislation or discover, somehow, that a stream so toxic that its water corroded irrigation pipes was natural. As absurd as the facts made it appear, the choice of judicial manipulation over democratic politics may have been inescapable. Legislation shifting property rights from agricultural to industrial interests would have been difficult in the context of nineteenth-century America, but not because the wholesale statutory destruction of property rights is generally impossible or even unusual. On the contrary, it has occurred repeatedly throughout American legal history.

Perhaps the earliest and most consequential was the Non-Intercourse Act of 1793 whereby Congress prohibited American Indians from selling land to anyone but the federal government.[22] When purchasers from the Indians claimed that both natural law and the Constitution prohibited the diminution of Indian property rights, Chief Justice Marshall in *Johnson* v. *M'Intosh* acknowledged that "the principles of abstract justice, which the Creator of all things has impressed on the mind of his creature man, and which are admitted to regulate, in a great degree, the rights of civilized nations" could not and would not be the deciding rules in the case. Instead he upheld the statute on the inevitable, if rarely articulated, ground that "Conquest gives a title which the Courts of the conqueror cannot deny."[23]

22 The act reads in pertinent part, "[N]o purchase or grant of lands, or of any title or claim thereto, from any Indians or nation or tribe of Indians, within the bounds of the United States, shall be of any validity in law or equity, unless the same be made by a treaty or a convention entered into pursuant to the constitution ..." Act of March 1, 1793, Pub. L. No. 2–19, § 8, 1 Stat. 329, 330.

23 *Johnson* v. *M'Intosh*, 21 US 543 (1823). To be precise, *Johnson* held that the practice of prohibiting the Indians' transfer of land to anyone other than the sovereign had existed since the beginning of the age of discovery and therefore the Non-Intercourse Act had simply codified preexisting practice, rather than created new law. It is important to note that Marshall stressed that the conquered would not always lose their property rights because "humanity" requires that "the conquered shall not be wantonly oppressed, and [should be] incorporated with the victorious nation, and become subjects or citizens of the government with which they are connected. The new and old members of the society mingle with each other; the distinction between them is gradually lost, and they make one people." Marshall concluded, however, that such incorporation was impossible in the context of the United States in the eighteenth and nineteenth centuries. See Maria E. Montoya, *Translating Property Rights: The Maxwell Land Grant and the Conflict over Land in the American West, 1840–1900* (Berkeley: University of California Press, 2002). See also Stuart Banner, *How the Indians Lost their Land: Law and Power on the Frontier* (Cambridge: Harvard University Press, 2005). Banner argues that British and American policy up to *Johnson* had recognized full property rights in Indians and that their land had been acquired not on the basis of conquest as proclaimed by Marshal but by purchase. Banner stresses, however, that attention to the use of law should not distract one from the coercion at the core of the process: "The threat of physical force was always present, but most of the time it could be kept out of view, because most of the time it was not needed."

Similar legislative directness and judicial candor were not likely to work in *Sanderson*, however, for two important reasons. First, unlike Native Americans, agricultural interests were not politically powerless. There were a lot of farmers and the males could vote. But even if it had been politically feasible to take away agriculture's right to clean water, the legislature would have faced the possibility of judicial review for unconstitutionally taking property rights. Federal and state constitutions require both that a deprivation of property be done for a public use and that the owner be justly compensated. Unlike the Indians, the farmers were part of the conquerors, not the conquered, and a clear legislative declaration that existing property rights were being destroyed might paradoxically have made it more difficult for the Pennsylvania Supreme Court to approve their destruction. While transparency and honesty in judicial institutions may be a stable tenet of rule-of-law rhetoric, it simply was not available in this instance.

So Justice Clark, in stark contrast to Chief Justice Marshall, wrote an intellectually dishonest opinion and declared a highly toxic Meadow Brook to be natural. First, he stated the ground norm: "The defendants, being the owners of the land, had a right to mine the coal." The opinion then turns to the knotty issue of naturalness:

> It will be observed that the defendants have done nothing to change the character of the water, or to diminish its purity, save what results from the natural use and enjoyment of their own property. They have brought nothing onto the land artificially. The water as it is poured into Meadow brook is the water which the mine naturally discharged. Its impurity arises from natural, not artificial, causes.

The contrast between artificial and natural is the leitmotiv of the opinion:

> A drift [mine shaft] is in some sense an artificial opening in the land, and accumulates and discharges water in a greater volume and extent than would otherwise result from purely natural causes; yet mining by drift has ... been held to be a natural user of the land. So, too, we think, according to the present practice of mining, the working of the lower strata by shaft ... must be considered the natural user of the land ...; and, as the water cannot be discharged by gravity alone, it must necessarily ... be lifted to the surface by artificial means, and thence be discharged through the ordinary natural channels for the drainage of the county.

Banner, 82–3. In this sense, the dispossession of the Indians resembles an accelerated version of the enclosures, allowing white Americans to displace an entire population but consider it entirely just.

Once the reader accepts Clark's characterization of "nature," his logic becomes impregnable. Since mining is the natural use of coal lands, it follows that the water accumulated in the shafts is there naturally, and since the defendants brought nothing onto the land, the resulting pollution is also natural. The only remaining problem was the "lift[ing] to the surface by artificial means," i.e., the use of pumps to remove the water from the shafts and discharge it into the brook, but the court dealt with the issue by assuming that some of the polluted water would have reached the Meadow Brook "by the mere force of gravity, naturally, and without any fault of the defendants." If so, it follows that the additional polluted water produced by pumping would only be adding insult to an injury already caused by naturally polluted water flowing naturally out of the mine by force of natural gravity alone.

Judicial Sophistry, Political Legitimacy, and Social Change

The nineteenth century was a time when US judges acted not only to enforce the law but also to facilitate social change. Whether condemned as subsidizing industry and the wealthy – an American version of the enclosures' revolution of the rich against the poor – or extolled as cutting the Gordian knot of transaction costs, the judges' goal was economic growth, and changing the preexisting property law was an important means to that end:

> As the spirit of economic development began to take hold of American society in the early years of the nineteenth century, ... the idea of property underwent a fundamental transformation – from a static agrarian conception entitling an owner to undisturbed enjoyment, to a dynamic, instrumental, and more abstract view of property that emphasized the newly paramount virtues of productive use and development.[24]

Although unique in its twists and turns, the *Sanderson* cases illustrate this shift well. *Sanderson I* embodied the type of law that we are taught to admire and strive to create. It enforced doctrine, or as Scalia phrased it, "the rule of law as a law of rules."[25] The Sandersons had a property right to clean water; they had invested on the expectation that their right would be enforced; and

[24] Horwitz, *Transformation*, 31. See also Nelson, *Americanization*, 162: "Recognition of exclusive property rights in accordance with traditional doctrines would have made economic development impossible, now that scarcity of resources and new forms of technology had produced an economy in which initial developers were not always utilizing economic resources in the manner most profitable to society as a whole; accordingly, the traditional doctrines were rejected."

[25] Antonin Scalia, "The Rule of Law as a Law of Rules," *University of Chicago Law Review* 56 (1989): 1175.

the court did precisely what they expected and, indeed, had a *right* to. This is the recipe not only for justice for the Sandersons but also, at least according to orthodox wisdom, for economic growth and social progress. Yet, as we have seen, by *Sanderson IV*, Judge Stanton's initial dismissal of the plaintiffs' property rights in the Luzerne County Court of Common Pleas that the Supreme Court overturned in *Sanderson I* had become the law, and industry had been freed of the preexisting property doctrines that threatened to strangle it in the cradle. Understanding how that transformation was achieved and especially how it was done legitimately requires us to step back from the opinions themselves and examine their context and effect.

In the first place, the process was political, not legal. The eight years between *Sanderson I* in 1878 and *IV* in 1886 did not reflect a doctrinal change of heart by the judges of the Pennsylvania Supreme Court; it was the result of the political reshaping of that court. While the court seemed to have reversed itself, it was in fact not the same court, but one in which three of the seven justices had changed. What had been a six-to-one victory for the Sandersons became a four-to-three victory for the coal company. And that change can be attributed principally to one man.

Henry M. Hoyt was an imposing former Union general as well as a prominent Republican Party lawyer.[26] A native of Luzerne County, he was hired by the Pennsylvania Coal Company to represent their interests in the first iteration of the case. Hoyt was unavailable for *Sanderson II* and *III* as he was serving as governor of Pennsylvania. Being limited to one term, he returned to the bar in 1883 to again represent the coal company, this time in *Sanderson IV* before a Supreme Court that included three new justices, all either close friends or political allies, Justices James P. Sterrett, Henry Green, and the author of *Sanderson IV*, Silas M. Clark.

Justice Sterrett was appointed in 1877 by a Republican and then elected to the court in 1878 on the same ticket that made Hoyt governor.[27] In 1879, Hoyt appointed Justice Green to succeed Justice Woodward, the stalwart defender of property rights and author of *Sanderson I*, who had died.[28] The election of 1882 brought Justice Clark, a compromise Democratic candidate from the heavily coal-supported Indiana County.[29] So when Hoyt came before the court in *Sanderson IV* with substantially the same arguments he had made eight years prior, he found himself, to put it mildly, before a more receptive court.

[26] Gov. Henry M. Hoyt, available at www.portal.state.pa.us/portal/server.pt/community/1879-1951/4284/henry_martyn_hoyt/468314.

[27] Frank M. Eastman, *Courts and Lawyers of Pennsylvania: A History* (New York, 1922), 514.

[28] Ibid. 515.

[29] Ibid.

The "rule of law" problems with the *Sanderson* cases do not end with their baldly political nature. Marshall's opinion in *Johnson* v. *M'Intosh* was every bit as politically instrumental. Indeed, Marshall's "Conquest gives a title which the Courts of the conqueror cannot deny" reminds one more of Mao Zedong's "power comes from the barrel of a gun" than it does our usual jurisprudential fare. But Marshall's opinion has a moral and intellectual honesty that Clark's sorely lacks. He told the truth, injustice and all. Anyone reading the opinion in the twenty-first century cannot help but be as moved by the opinion as Marshall clearly was anguished in its authorship almost 200 years earlier. A coal baron of the late nineteenth-century reading *Sanderson IV*, on the other hand, might feel only contentment that justice was done. Even a disinterested Pennsylvanian, although perhaps not persuaded by Clark's characterization of pollution as natural, was unlikely to realize the profound change that the opinion represented. In other words, Marshall was straightforward and honest in recognizing not only what was being sacrificed but also how and why it was being lost. Clark, by contrast, was not only deceptive and manipulative but even scolded the Sandersons for greedily trying to stifle a "great public industry" to avoid a "mere personal inconvenience."

But does this mean that we should applaud Marshall's transparency and condemn Clark's obfuscation? If one takes the Panglossian perspective of a legal system where the legal rules are clear, judges are not only competent and honest but also either ignorant of or indifferent to the context and consequences of their actions, and the legislature, the bureaucracy, the police, and other legal institutions operate as middle-school civics textbooks portray them – where, in short, all five of Demsetz's contrafactual assumptions are fulfilled – then the answer must be yes. In that imaginary world, we can afford the ideological satisfaction of a transparent judiciary, although of course if we lived in such a world, we wouldn't need a judiciary. For better or worse, however, legal systems don't work that way any more often than markets do, i.e., they never work that way, and in an imperfect world our goal for the judiciary may be to facilitate progress with the least social cost.

While it would be silly to ascribe this high-toned motive to Governor Hoyt and his judicial allies, the effect of the *Sanderson IV* decision may have approximated this result. It shifted property rights and wealth from politically entrenched agricultural interests to more productive industrial ones and did so without sacrificing the system's legitimacy. If Clark had been as candid as Marshall in *Johnson*, it is unlikely that society in general, much less agricultural interests, would have accepted the necessity of their imposed sacrifice. More likely would have been a political stalemate with eventually the same result but accompanied by de-legitimation of the political and legal systems that provide social order. The 1952–3 Arizona case(s) of *Bristor* v. *Cheatham* can illustrate the potential cost of such candor.[30]

Like *Sanderson*, *Bristor* was a water case where a state supreme court destroyed property rights to respond to economic and technological change. The prevailing water law doctrine in Arizona then and now was prior appropriation. Unlike the riparian doctrines of natural flow and reasonable use that characterize Pennsylvania and other water-rich eastern states, prior appropriation severs water from its appurtenant land, considers it a public resource, and makes it available for appropriation by whoever first puts it to beneficial use. The doctrinal and practical differences are stark. In riparian jurisdictions, the owner of the adjacent land has a property right in the use of the water as an inherent incident of ownership of the land. Under prior appropriation, riparian ownership gives no rights to adjacent water. Instead, ownership of the water is acquired by prior beneficial use by any member of the public. The result is a highly regulated regime of water rights with elaborate schedules of priority determined by date of initial beneficial use.

The sole exception to prior appropriation was ground water, which was the focus in *Bristor*. Underground water had been unimportant and ignored when Arizona created its prior appropriation regime in the nineteenth century, and so, by the time pump technology provided easy and cheap access to ground water, the Arizona Supreme Court, in 1904, applied the existing common-law *ad coelum* doctrine that gave "absolute ownership" of ground water to the owner of the surface land. In sharp contrast to all other water resources, which were public and heavily regulated, ground water was private and totally unrestricted. As surface water supplies dwindled and ever more powerful pumps depleted underground aquifers, however, a broad range of interest groups called for legislation to regulate the "mining" of ground water. Although by the 1940s agriculture was a declining part of the economy, opposition from concentrated interests, especially from cotton growers, consistently blocked effective legislation. The stage was set for *Bristor I*.

Like the Sandersons, Bristor and his fellow plaintiffs were trying to protect the established use of contested water. If it had been surface water, their priority would have protected them, but it was ground water, meaning that defendant Cheatham could take whatever his pumps could bring to the surface. Backed by several powerful *amici curiae*, including the state Attorney General, residential developers, and older agricultural interests with existing

30 *Bristor* v. *Cheatham I*, 73 Ariz. 228, 240 P. 2d 185 (1952), and *Bristor* v. *Cheatham II*, 75 Ariz. 227, 255 P. 2d 173 (1953). For background, see Dean E. Mann, "Law and Politics of Ground Water in Arizona," *Arizona Law Review* 2 (1960): 241, and Walter Rusinek, "Conflict over Ground Water in Arizona," *Arizona and the West* 27:2 (1985): 143.

wells, the plaintiffs persuaded the court in a 3–2 decision of January 12, 1952, to declare ground water public and subject to prior appropriation.

Like Marshall in *M'Intosh*, the *Bristor I* majority faced the issue squarely. Noting that new pump technology had exacerbated an existing crisis, they declared that "[t]o permit the present underground water race to continue unabated, without regulation or control, would inevitably lead to exhaustion of the underground water supply and consequently to economic disaster" [235]. Alluding to the prior wholesale destruction of *ad coelum* air rights to accommodate aviation, they did not disguise that for them changes in technology and economics demanded concomitant changes in property law:

> The common-law concept that the owner of land owned everything to the center of the earth below and to the sky above became a part of the body of that law under conditions wholly different from those which obtain anywhere today. In fact scientific advancement has made it wholly inapplicable to present conditions.

The response was immediate and apocalyptic. Justice Arthur La Prade's dissent likened the majority decision to "the dropping of a gigantic atomic bomb in our midst" and warned that "its impact on the economy of this state will be so vast and devastating that no one at this time can envision its effect" [243]. But it was not solely the economic impact that outraged La Prade and others. Property rights must be maintained, even if inefficient:

> Where a principle of law has become settled ..., it is binding on the courts and should be followed ... [I]t is the duty of the court ... to adhere to such decisions without regard to how it might be inclined to decide if the question were new ... The rule that such final decisions will ordinarily be adhered to even when they are *erroneous applies to decisions relating to real property with particular force*. [Emphasis in original]

La Prade had allies, although probably more for his economic alarm than his jurisprudential concerns. The Farmer's Defense Association, originally formed to oppose the extension of child labor laws to the cotton fields, immediately started a well-funded campaign for a rehearing. Political pressure grew – including threats of physical harm to the majority justices – and by the end of February, just weeks after *Bristor I*, the court had granted a rehearing. By the next March when the court reversed its decision in *Bristor II*, again by 3–2, no one was surprised. Chief Justice Rawghlie Clemont Stanford, a former governor described "as a loyal friend often unable to refuse favors," had switched his vote and absolute ownership of percolating ground water was safe.[31]

[31] Rusinek, "Conflict over Ground Water," 156.

What followed was not only the accelerated depletion of ground water but also continued political stalemate. Despite a broad consensus that absolute ownership of ground water threatened to stall Arizona's development, legislative action came to a standstill, "a complete impasse was reached."[32] It was not until the Ground Water Management Act of 1980 that the legislature was able to act. By that time, the shift from rural to urban had been completed, and the Supreme Court had little trouble rejecting the inevitable property rights-based challenge.[33] As one commentator put it, the court simply "swept away eighty years of precedent" and summarily "dismissed the notion that landowners held a property right to the water under their land."[34] The destruction of property rights attempted initially in *Bristor I* had been completed, but there was no outcry. Indeed "most residents were unaware that it had happened."[35] Times had changed, and the law had finally caught up.

The point is not whether Arizona would have been better off – or, in our terms, whether it would have developed more successfully – if *Bristor I* had prevailed. Sooner or later unfettered private ownership of ground water had to be destroyed, if not through the democratic process, then through judicial action, and eventually it was. What is important for us is that *Bristor I* and *Sanderson IV* represent two contrasting judicial approaches to changing the status quo. The former addressed the underlying issue directly and was forthright in its value judgments. It failed. The latter dissembled and succeeded.

Sophistry will not always be necessary, of course. If the legal owner has no power, like American Indians, honesty and transparency are available. Similarly, if little will be lost and the aggregate gains are great, the process is likely to be smooth even if the destruction of property rights is clear. Such was not only the case by 1980 with underground water in Arizona but also when Congress destroyed the *ad coelum* air rights of every land owner in the United States with the Air Commerce Act of 1926 and the Civil Aeronautics Act of 1938.[36] It was also the reason that little fuss was made in 1998 when the Ninth Circuit Court of Appeals ruled in *Panavision* that cyber-squatter Dennis Toeppen's properly registered internet domain name "panavision.com" was invalid because it was done in "bad faith," as if, all of a sudden, the federal

[32] Mann, "Law and Politics," 262.

[33] *Town of Chino* v. *Prescott* 131 Ariz. 78, 638 P. 2d. 1324 (1981).

[34] Rusinek, "Conflict over Ground Water," 161.

[35] Ibid. 162.

[36] Pub. L. No. 69–254, 44 Stat. 568 and ch. 601, 52 Stat. 973 (codified as amended in scattered sections of 49 USC, including 49 USC § 401 (1940)) respectively. Cited and discussed in Troy A. Rule, "Airspace in an Age of Drones," *Boston University Law Review* 95 (2015): 155, 166–7.

judiciary had decided that a valid property right depended on the normative acceptability of one's motives.[37]

The real explanation, of course, was not morality but economics. The right of a landowner to block high altitude overflights and the right of an opportunistic cyber squatter to prevent corporations from using trade names on the internet were socially worthless. They may have been property rights in the abstract world of law, but once they threatened the productive exploitation of new technology, they were easily eliminated. But these exemplify the myriad easy cases, the destruction of property rights that not even property rights advocates notice. It is when property law protects real interests, however obsolete or inefficient, that a society may need the artifice that characterized *Sanderson*.

LAW, PROPERTY RIGHTS, AND CREATIVE DESTRUCTION

As we look back at the enclosure movement and nineteenth-century US water law, no magic formula emerges but a few conclusions seem beyond dispute. First, what was lost was the legal and social framework of property entitlements protecting existing productive activities and ways of living. Second, the old property regime was discarded to allow society to respond to opportunities for new wealth. Third, the end result of both processes was net social progress, at the very least from the perspective of the time.

One can disagree about the normative value of both phenomena. The fate of the serfs/freemen and others at the bottom was brutal by any standard, and even the copyholders saw their lives transformed involuntarily and rarely for the better. *Sanderson* too is a decidedly mixed bag, especially in retrospect as we face the long-term cost of industrial pollution, and anyone concerned with the judicial role will balk at the celebration of judges bending the law to serve the interests of the powerful. Furthermore, the total denial of the Sandersons' property rights may not have been necessary. The court might have limited coal mining to areas less immediately damaging to agrarian interests or used its equitable powers to declare an injunction unavailable in the circumstances but reinstated a limited measure of damages. Indeed, subsequent Pennsylvania cases "whittled" the *Sanderson* holding down by "ingenious quibbles" just as post-*Gateward's Case* courts had done two-and-a-half centuries earlier.[38]

37 *Panavision I*, 938 F. Supp. 616 (C. C. Cal. 1996), aff'd 141 F.3d 1316 (9th Cir. 1998). See also *Kremen* v. *Cohen*, 337 F.3d 1024 (2003) (holding that domain names are a form of intangible property for the Californian tort of conversion).

38 See N.I.S.G., "Mines – Natural Use – Limitation of the Sanderson Case," *University of Pennsylvania Law Review* 62:3 (1913–1914): 212. That courts are capable of innovative remedies designed to accommodate legal justice and economic growth is exemplified by two

Nonetheless, few would wish to return to the subsistence agriculture of sixteenth-century England or even bucolic eighteenth-century America. At this point, therefore, it may be time to turn our gaze away from what was lost – the settled expectations of stable societies – and look instead at what was created. First, of course, was the massive increase in material wellbeing as new property regimes accelerated growth. That alone may outweigh the personal losses from a utilitarian perspective, but more was created than material progress. Although these cases destroyed economically obsolete property entitlements, they did so in a manner that neither significantly weakened the social structure nor threatened regime legitimacy. Indeed, the opposite is true. Both the enclosures and the transformation of nineteenth-century US law created new stable property rights that became the ideological foundations for more productive regimes.

And ideology is important. As we've already seen, North identified an appropriate ideology as the basis of the normative order needed for markets to operate, and considered it more important than the content of the formal rules themselves. On the political dimension, Barrington Moore saw the enclosures as nothing less than a bridge to democracy. Enclosure liberated the mass of the English population from stifling feudal relationships that may have provided economic security at a low level but would never have become the basis of democratic development. Moreover, the legal nature of the villagers' dispossession, with its occasional victory of the weak over the strong, was a form of political education. It failed to protect the weak in the long run – indeed the law was the central vehicle for their dispossession – but it delayed the deprivation and legitimated the legal system in the process.

Karl Polanyi characterized the positive side of this superficially cynical process well:

> Why should the ultimate victory of a trend be taken as a proof of the ineffectiveness of the efforts to slow down its progress? And why should the purpose of these measures not be seen precisely in that which they achieved, i.e., in the slowing down of the rate of change? That which is ineffectual in stopping a line of development altogether is not, on that account, altogether ineffectual.[39]

E. P. Thompson went further and argued that the use of the law by the lords to exclude the commoners created the rule of law itself, which he proclaimed "a cultural achievement of universal significance":[40]

---

celebrated twentieth-century US nuisance cases, *Boomer* v. *Atlantic Cement*, 26 N.Y.2d 219, 309 N.Y.2d 312, 257 N.E.2d 870 (1970), and *Spur* v. *Del Webb*, 108 Ariz. 178, 494 P.2d 700 (1972).

39 Polanyi, *Great Transformation*, 36.

40 Thompson, *Whigs and Hunters: The Origin of the Black Act* (New York: Pantheon, 1975), 264.

> [I]mmense efforts were made to project the image of a ruling class which was itself subject to the rule of law, and whose legitimacy rested upon the equity and universality of those forms. The rulers were, in serious senses, whether willingly or unwillingly, the prisoners of their own rhetoric; they played the games of power according to rules that suited them, but they could not break those rules or the whole game would be thrown away.[41]

No one has described *Sanderson* or the transformation of nineteenth-century American law in quite such elevated terms. Critics from the left recognize common-law judges' innovative role, but regret what they argue was an unjust redistribution of wealth. Those taking a more economic perspective, see the legal changes as simply eliminating transaction costs and allowing the market to operate as markets should. Neither side seemed to regret the departure from doctrine. Even Stephen F. Williams, a strong advocate of property rights, who later became a federal circuit court judge, seemed to take efficient property rights as an expected destination for all societies: "[I]t seems scarcely credible that society could long exist without viewing a goal of maximizing aggregate utility ... as at least *relevant*" to judicial interpretation.[42] A third view sees a political silver lining in the liberation from inhibiting social structures and not only for capitalists:

> In the colonial period the expectation had been that all men would share the same values, and criminal prosecutions were frequently brought against those who refused to abide by the values that the community accepted. By the nineteenth century few expected all men to embrace the same values, and criminal prosecutions were rarely brought for breach of ethical codes.[43]

Whatever one's normative judgment, the process was the same: The change was profound, often unjust, but accomplished without the violence and dislocation that would have rendered the losers' lives even worse.

It is here that we can find relevance to current issues in law and development. To get rich – or at least less poor – today's poorest countries must be able to transform their societies and economies to respond to growth opportunities in ways functionally similar to what England and the United States did long ago. Their existing economic structures must be destroyed and replaced by new more productive ones. As we will see with China, law is not necessary, but the enclosure movement and *Sanderson* demonstrate its potentially positive role, ironically not in protecting "archaic" property rights but in legitimating the process of their replacement with "rational" ones.

41 Ibid. 263.
42 Williams, "Book Review," 1202. Emphasis in the original.
43 Nelson, *Americanization*, 164.

The human effects of the enclosures and of the industrialization of the United States were revolutionary, but the processes were not. They were legal, not violent. Lives were fundamentally changed, many for the worse, but few were lost in bloody conflict. Change was gradual, not immediate; victims' futures were lost, but many could cling to their presents and had time to adjust to their new futures. Perhaps most important, the processes were presented as the legitimate operation of a preexisting system; in fact, they *were* part of the system. In both instances, the law was changed by and for the benefit of the strong, but not by a straightforward declaration of victory, but through a process that protected, if only partially, cynically, and temporarily, the material and, equally important, dignitary interests of the weak.

We have focused so far on how British commoners and American farmers lost their property rights so that the larger society could respond to new economic opportunities. In the Chinese and Cambodian case studies of Chapters 5 and 6, we will see how that process continues today. But property rights and their destruction inevitably have political as well as economic functions, and not simply as the means of pursuing economic goals as exemplified by *Sanderson* and the enclosures. In the next chapter, therefore, we examine one instance of the destruction of property rights expressly to achieve political ends: postwar Japan's elimination of its landlord class. Just as economically driven change inevitably has political consequences, however, we will see that politically motivated change has its own economic consequences, and not necessarily for the better.

4

Property and Politics

Japan

In the previous chapter, we saw how the English and American legal systems changed property law to allow powerful landowners to exploit economic opportunities that would otherwise have been prevented by existing property rights. Both events had political effects, but their impetus and motivation were economic. The landowners wanted to introduce new technologies or products to meet emerging market demand in ways that would illegally harm their neighbors. Legal institutions were used to steal from the weak. In this chapter, we shift from an economic to a political perspective as we examine land reform in post-WW II Japan. Here politics dominated from the outset and legal institutions were used to steal from the strong.

Postwar Japan, intentionally or not, chose a politically stable rural population over an efficient agricultural sector. The core principle of the next five decades of agricultural policy was to guarantee ownership of farm land by those who farmed it, first by a comprehensive land reform, later by severely restricting the rural land market to prevent the reemergence of tenancy. On its own terms, the policy was an unequivocal success. Rural Japan became a central pillar of postwar Japanese democracy. Looked at through an economic lens, however, the picture is very different.

The story begins with the legal restructuring of Japanese agriculture in the latter half of the nineteenth century. Already highly commercialized but faced with Western pressure to modernize its legal system, Japan shifted from a nominally feudal land tenure system to a thoroughly capitalist one by the end of the century, a change that was accompanied by increased tenancy and the emergence of a class of absentee landlords. Although the causes and magnitude of the transformation are debated, the conventional wisdom in the immediate postwar period was that rapacious landlords had so exploited their tenants that the xenophobia of the latter became one of the prime causes of Japanese militarism and World War II. It followed that, pressed by the American Occupation, an initially reluctant government passed a thorough land reform that was intended to replace the easily manipulated downtrodden tenants of prewar Japan with a rural cadre of enlightened liberal farmers that would preside over a renewed blooming of Japanese agriculture. As we shall see, it did not quite work out that way: the newly independent owners became not only reliable supporters of conservative political parties but also fierce defenders of a protectionist regime that has led to one of the world's least productive agricultural sectors.

PREWAR JAPAN'S TENANCY PROBLEM

For the more than 250 years of the Tokugawa Period (1603–1867) before Japan opened to the West, it was illegal to sell land.[1] Indeed, from a legal perspective there was no private ownership of land at all since the ideological basis of land possession was feudal, not liberal. Nor was economic growth or a market economy more than tolerated; the regime's goal was stasis, not growth. Such was the official ideology and legal form; the social and economic reality was quite different.[2] By the nineteenth century, Japan was a wealthy, commercialized country with a productive agricultural sector and an established, if *de facto*, market in collateralized interests in agricultural land if not in title per se.[3]

In 1868, when the Meiji regime (1867–1912) replaced feudal tenure with freely alienable individualized title to the farmers "customarily considered to be in possession,"[4] therefore, it changed less on the ground than it did in the law books. It was nonetheless the first step in the conversion of a nominally precommercial legal system into one that was fully capitalist by the end of the century. The second step was a series of cadastral surveys intended to clarify ownership and uncover land that had previously been untaxed. The result was a 48 percent increase in registered land and the implementation of a land tax that provided the bulk of revenues to the Meiji state in its first decades.

The reforms were a mixed bag for the farmers. Many were confirmed in their ownership of their land and their ability to sell it, and the ending of feudalism legally freed them from involuntary ties both to agriculture and to local feudal superiors. These advantages were frequently outweighed by other factors, however. First, as with the enclosure movement, only one form of

1 Keiji Owada, *Hisshi nihon no nōchi kaikaku [Secret History of Agricultural Land Reform in Japan]* (Tokyo: Nihon Keizai Shimbun, 1981), 11.

2 Ibid. 11.

3 Thomas C. Smith, *The Agrarian Origins of Modern Japan* (Palo Alto, CA: Stanford University Press, 1959), 104–6.

4 Ronald P. Dore, *Land Reform in Japan* (New York: Schocken, 1959), 14. Owada, *Secret History*, 12.

legal ownership, unified title in a single entity, was recognized, which meant that all other rights were eliminated, including, most importantly, a longstanding form of permanent tenancy.[5] There were also disputes in the attribution of ownership, and mortgagees rather than cultivators sometimes received the title deed, converting customary owner-debtors into formal tenants. Adding to this distress for both farmer-owners and tenants was the conversion of what had been flexible in-kind taxes and rents into nominally fixed monetary payments. These and other consequences of the increased commercialization of agriculture led to a decline in the proportion of independent proprietors (by the 1890s, they constituted only about a third of Japanese farmers) and an increase in the proportion of tenanted land from about 30 percent at the beginning of the Meiji Period to 45 percent by the first decade of the twentieth century.[6]

The Meiji Landlord and Rural Social Structure

It was the assumed political consequences of this increased tenancy that became the impetus for the postwar land reform, but the causal link from late nineteenth-century social trends to political events five decades later was not as linear as American and Japanese reformers thought. Although the tenancy disputes that were present throughout the Tokugawa Period continued into the Meiji, the nature of Japanese agriculture and rural society and particularly the role of most landlords lessened the initial impact of full commercialization.[7] Relative to other crops, wet rice agriculture

5 See Masatoshi Osawa, *Nōchishoyuuken no riron to tenkai [The Theory and Development of Property Rights in Agricultural Land]* (Tokyo: Seibunsho, 2005), 49. The elimination of this tenancy led to such social discontent that it was re-established by the 1898 Civil Code. Dore, *Land Reform*, 16.

6 Osawa, *Theory and Development*, 16 and 32. The cause of the increase in tenanted land is disputed. Smethurst has argued that the development of new agricultural land, not impoverishment and foreclosure, was the major cause. See Richard J. Smethurst, *Agricultural Development and Tenancy Disputes in Japan, 1870–1940* (Princeton: Princeton University Press, 1986). See Yoshiaki Nishida, "Growth of the Meiji Landlord System and Tenancy Disputes after World War I: A Critique of Richard Smethurst, Agricultural Development and Tenancy Disputes in Japan, 1870–1940," and Smethurst, "A Challenge to Orthodoxy and Its Orthodox Critics: A Reply to Nishida Yoshiaki," *The Journal of Japanese Studies* 15:2 (1989), 389 and 417 respectively. For a more legal and economic perspective sympathetic to Smethurst, see Mark Ramseyer, "The Fable of Land Reform: Leases and Credit Markets in Occupied Japan," *Journal of Economics & Management Strategy* 24:4 (2015): 934.

7 The courts were another mitigating factor. The Daishin'in or Great Court of Cassation, the highest appellate court for private law, frequently sided with tenants in disputes with owners in disputes over the legal nature and validity of traditional forms of leaseholds, thus delaying the social impact of agricultural commercialization. The passage of the new Civil Code in 1899, however, strengthened the owners' legal position and weakened the courts' ability to favor

rewards intensive inputs of labor per acre, is difficult to scale or mechanize, and is thus conducive to large numbers of people working a small amount of land. Of course, in regions of high labor costs and cheap land, such as California, rice cultivation is both extensive and mechanized. The situation in Meiji Japan, however, was precisely the opposite: land was limited and labor was abundant. As a result, when Japanese farmers became overextended and lost their land to creditors, which was an increasing pattern, it was more productive for the new owner to keep the farmer in place as a tenant than to take over direct management of the land and either employ the dispossessed farmer as agricultural labor or allow him to leave for the city and become an urban proletarian, the fate of many villagers during the English enclosures.

Close ties between landlords and tenants also fit the social and ideological conditions of nineteenth-century rural Japan. Japan's mountainous topography meant that villages were often politically, economically, and socially isolated. The particular requirements of wet rice agriculture reinforced village solidarity and interdependence. Without cooperation, the village could not construct, maintain, or operate the complicated irrigation systems upon which paddy farming depends. Add to these physical conditions the fact that the landlord was himself a farmer with whom the new tenant had strong personal connections and who came from the same social and cultural background, and the overtly exploitative aspects of increased tenancy were substantially softened. Physical proximity and community networks were reinforced by the paternalistic Neo-Confucian philosophy that had dominated Tokugawa ideology and that the Meiji government made the core of its aggressive program of universal basic education. Whether inherent in the philosophical tenets of the *Analects* or an instrumental artifact of the productive relations of the Meiji village described above, the Meiji version of Neo-Confucianism stressed precisely the harmony, unity, and deference that wet rice agriculture in the nineteenth century demanded.

What came out of this geographical, technological, ideological, and social mix was a form of tenancy that, although rapidly increasing during the early and middle parts of Meiji, posed surprisingly little political threat to the regime or to social harmony. At the center was the Meiji landlord. This excerpt from an 1893 tenancy contract illustrates the primary characteristics of the system:

traditional over modern forms of possession and ownership. See Yuka Kaneko, "New Trends in Land Dispute Resolution in Asia: Interaction between Formal and Informal Forums," unpublished paper, 14–7.

To Otaki Saburoemon [landlord]:

[Description and Designation of the land ... Rent ... Surcharge ...]

I hereby certify that, from this year and for such times as the relationship between us shall last, I have undertaken tenancy of the above land. I undertake to deliver, by 31 December each year, at such place as you shall direct, the above rent and surcharge [an additional 2% required to cover loss in shipping the rice to market] in selected [specific quality] rice, carefully and conscientiously baled.

I beg that in years of bad harvest through natural causes you will, on inspection of the crop, make such reduction in rent as seems to you fit. In the case, however, of a fall in yields resulting from my own bad management and affecting myself alone, I undertake to ask for no reduction in rent. I shall, of course, make no attempt to sell the right of tenancy, nor be indolent in cultivation of the land, nor engage in any other unjust conduct. In the event that I should break the contract, guarantor will pay full compensation. In such circumstance, or, indeed, at any other time, I undertake to raise no single word of complaint should you, as your convenience makes necessary, decide to terminate my tenancy.

[Signed]
Tenant ...
Guarantor ...[8]

The Otaki family was an example of what Ronald Dore has called "paternalistic" landlords. Paternalistic they may have been, but as the contract illustrates, they left little to sentiment. To begin with, there was a formal and comprehensive written document. As compared to the oral leases of the Tokugawa, this relationship was formed within a legal framework. The land, rent, surcharge, quality and condition of rice, and time and place of delivery were clearly stipulated, and the tenant waived any right to convey his tenancy. But the contract goes on to describe a subservience that runs counter to what one might expect in a wholly commercialized agreement. It formalizes a relationship based on benevolence, and the Otaki family apparently lived up to that expectation as a contemporaneous account describes:

[The Otakis] grew rich, but they did not let it go to their heads. Unlike the landlords of neighboring districts they did not ape town manners. The master did not keep a mistress. He did not buy a bowler hat. Nor did he grow a moustache. He did not build a lavishly expensive garden. He grew *bonsai* as a hobby, but tended them himself. He wore "long clothes" – the mark of a leisured gentleman – only for weddings and funerals.[9]

8 Dore, *Land Reform*, 33. Dore divides non-absentee Meiji landlords into paternalistic, paternalistic-progressive, paternalistic-progressive-didactic, and the modern non-paternalistic landlords. *Land Reform*, 25–53.

9 Ibid. 32.

It is important to understand the significance of the landlords' unassuming manner. It may have been an expression of relative equality, but it was also an instrument of economic and social dominance. In Otaki Saburoemon's village, forty of the forty-five households were his tenants. There is no doubt that Meiji landlords used their position for economic gain, but the interdependence of social and economic power meant that they also had to provide dignity and status to their tenants. The plea for rent reductions in bad times, therefore, was not simply Confucian rhetoric. Rent was high, but reductions were expected even in good years so that the landlord could consistently display his benevolence and emphasize that his family remained part of the community.

There were other advantages to the tenants' position as well. Rent was fixed and in kind, which meant that any additional production, including increases from additional fields brought into cultivation, was largely retained by the tenants. This meant that in times of generally increasing productivity the tenants did better, while in bad years they could count on greater rent reductions. Add to these financial features the fact that many landlords, those whom Dore calls the "paternalistic-progressive" and the "paternalistic-progressive-didactic" types, also made concerted efforts to improve their tenants' agricultural techniques and, in the latter case, their moral probity. Although the system was created by and for the landlord class, it spread the wealth effectively enough in good times – and a growing economy for most of this period meant more good times than bad – to maintain both social stability and increasing levels of agricultural production.

The Rise of Absentee Landlordism

The good times did not last, however, and neither did the landlord pattern described above. Even in the late Meiji Period, paternalistic landlords in more urbanized prefectures were being replaced by a more commercially oriented breed. Instead of being farmers themselves or at least living in the village, landlords were more likely to be city merchants or money lenders or former farmers who had moved to the city and, unlike Otaki Saburoemon, "let it go to their heads." Even many of those remaining in the village showed less concern for their tenants, as a contemporaneous complaint illustrates: "In one hamlet there are twenty-five landlords who devote themselves zealously to the tea ceremony, but only two or three who bother to encourage their tenants to build compost sheds."[10] Phony and self-serving as their Confucian parables about thrift, deference, and diligence might seem to twenty-first-century ears,

[10] Ibid. 69.

they were effective while their exponents lived in the village and tended their own *bonsai*. Once they moved to the city, had a mistress, sported a bowler, and wore long clothes, rhetoric could no longer disguise the economic one-sidedness of the relationship and agrarian conflict began to grow.[11]

But it was not just the decline in landlord virtue that led to the emergence of what eventually become known as the "problem of agriculture."[12] After the turn of the century and especially after World War I, ideological, social, and economic changes effectively doomed the Confucian system.[13] By 1918, the average head of a tenant household was no longer an illiterate farmer who had lived only in the village where he was born and had been indoctrinated to accept the Tokugawa system of hereditary social classes as the natural order of Japanese society. In 1872, just four years after the liberalization of land ownership, the Meiji government abolished all legal class distinctions other than the Imperial family and proclaimed formal equality before the law. Just as important, it instituted systems of compulsory education and universal conscription that made no distinction between the children of landlords and tenants. Thereafter, tenant children sat in the same classrooms and served in the same military as their richer neighbors (and everyone else), and the new ethics of citizenship, together with male villagers' experience beyond the village, benefited and constrained both landlords and tenants alike.[14]

When these social changes were exacerbated by global economic trends at the end of WW I, the system began to unravel. Although there had been stirrings of class consciousness earlier, a disastrous rice harvest in 1917, subsequent rice riots in 1918, the social disruption of rapid industrialization and urbanization, and the Great Depression's effect on agricultural prices combined to provide the material basis for a range of destabilizing populist ideologies. These ranged from Marxism on the left to *nōhonshugi* (agriculture as the essence), a Shinto nationalist ideology asserting the purity and virtue of Japanese rural life, on the xenophobic right. The result was increased unrest of a kind that was qualitatively different from the tenant revolts of the Tokugawa. Instead of demanding that an individual landlord live up to the virtuous standards of

[11] Osawa, *Theory and Development*, 33, and Owada, *Secret History*, 24.

[12] Dore, *Land Reform*, 89.

[13] There was a legal factor as well. The Civil Code of 1899 narrowed the range of legally recognized customary leaseholds and strengthened the Meiji regime's preference for formal ownership over traditional forms of possession. See Kaneko, "New Trends," 16. For a general overview of the jurisprudential background of both the Civil Code and the reaction to it, with special reference to land law, see Colin Jones, *Living Law in Japan: Social Jurisprudence in the Interwar Period*, dissertation presented for the PhD in history at Columbia University, September, 2017.

[14] Dore, *Land Reform*, 55.

Neo-Confucianism, the new disputes indicted the system as a whole, either because it violated new Western-derived egalitarian ideas or, from the opposite end of the political spectrum, because the system had deviated too far from the uniquely Japanese virtues of *nōhonshugi*.

The growth of dissatisfaction is dramatically reflected by the growth of tenancy disputes from 85 in 1917 to 6,824 in 1935.[15] These disputes were not isolated expressions of anger at individual landlords; nor were their demands limited to immediate relief from temporary distress. They were led by nationally organized tenant unions with systematically political goals. These unions, almost unknown at the end of the war, grew to nearly 5,000 by 1933 and exerted tight control over their members. For example, one union required each member to pledge:

1. Never to attempt to obtain tenancy rights of land already cultivated by another member by offering a higher rent.
2. Never to accept a landlord's demand to return land without consulting the union.
3. Never to relinquish tenancy rights without informing the union and arranging for another member to take over the land.
4. Never to take over the tenancy of land from another member without his agreement.
5. On purchasing land at present leased to another member, not to attempt to terminate the tenancy for at least one year.[16]

So much for the Confucian virtues of deference, loyalty, etc., at least rhetorically embraced by the Otaki tenants four decades earlier.

By the early 1930s, rural Japan, which had been a pillar of stability in the Meiji Period, had become the prime political challenge for the Tokyo regime, and while it may have seemed in the 1920s that the left would play a substantial role representing tenants, by the Manchurian Incident of 1931 and the start of the Sino-Japanese War, it was clear that Shinto nationalism would overwhelm the tenant unions and drive rural Japan into the obscurantism of *nōhonshugi*. Throughout the 1930s, the army and particularly the so-called "Young Officers" dedicated themselves to the restoration of mythic Japanese values in the countryside and became identified with the plight of poor farmers and allied with them against the evils of urban life. It was in the name of rural distress that they committed the series of assassinations that destroyed the last remnants of democratic government and that led, with each succeeding

[15] Ibid. 72.
[16] Ibid. 73.

incident, to more repressive and army-dominated cabinets until by the late 1930s militarism was firmly in control.

THE LAND REFORM

The failure of Japan's democratic governments in the 1920s and its descent into oppression at home and aggression abroad were more complex events than the account above. For one thing, the government recognized the need to reduce tenancy and had initiated legislation to address the issue before and during the war, with some success,[17] but what matters for our purposes is that both the victorious Americans and the defeated Japanese shared the belief that the social and economic collapse of rural Japan was the most powerful factor in Japanese militarism. Supreme Allied Commander Douglas MacArthur referred to prewar tenancy as a "condition approaching slavery," and the Soviet delegate to the Occupation stated that "it is well known that one of the main reasons of domination of reactionary chauvinistic military cliques has been the vitality of medieval survivals in the country and especially the presence of feudalistic oppression in the Japanese village."[18]

Although the exponents of a view of the Meiji landlord as a benevolent source of social stability might have argued precisely the reverse – that it was the *demise* of feudalism, not its rise, that led to rural collapse – the temper of the times was hardly conducive to the restoration of Neo-Confucianism. On the contrary, Japan's defeat saw almost immediate domestic calls for land reform, and with the passage of the Agricultural Land Law [ALL] in 1952, Japan "swept away the old tenancy system at a stroke" and created a class of owner-farmers that endures to this day.[19]

Initial Legislation

Reform began immediately. The first postwar Minister of Agriculture announced the government's intention to increase the number of owner-farmers in October, 1945, less than two months after the surrender, and by early December a bill had reached the Diet. Although moderate by the eventual standard of the ALL, the Diet members were not pleased. As one would

17 Kaneko, "New Trends," 18. Smethurst and others argue that general economic growth, opportunities to enter urban labor markets, and the reclamation of additional land meant that Japanese farmers, even those who cultivated primarily rented land, enjoyed generally improving standards of living from the beginning of the Meiji Period up to the 1930s.

18 Dore, *Land Reform*, 134 and 136.

19 Seiichi Tōbata, "Foreword" in Dore, *Land Reform*, ixxii.

expect from politicians elected in 1942 at the height of the war, they feared that even a mild weakening of the landlord class – the government draft would have affected only one-third of tenanted land – would threaten the traditional virtues of rural Japan and lead to political unrest and the rise of Marxist parties. "Why should landlords be singled out for such harsh treatment," asked one legislator. "Are they not equally children of the Emperor?"[20]

The resulting legislation, which was passed in late December 1945, not only left most tenancies untouched but also forced tenants to take the psychologically difficult first step of initiating land redistribution negotiations with their landlords, defined absentee landlord so narrowly that the village social structure remained intact, and calculated landholdings by individual, not household, so that landlords could multiply their acreage by parceling out ownership among their extended family. Perhaps most fundamental, 50 percent of the seats on the Agricultural Committees that were to implement the law at the village, prefectural, and central levels were reserved for landlords.

The landlords' partial victory did not last. New Diet elections in 1946 and increased Allied pressure to, in MacArthur's words, "tear from the soils of the Japanese countryside the blight of feudal landlordism" led to the Owner-Farmer Establishment Special Measures Law of October 21, 1946. All the obvious loopholes were eliminated. The amount of land allowed to be retained by landlords was reduced by 80 percent; households became the unit of ownership; direct negotiations between tenants and landlords were replaced by unilateral governmental purchase from landlords and resale to tenants; the definition of absentee landlord was broadened to include all landowners who did not normally reside in the village; and the composition of the Agricultural Committees was changed from 50 percent landlords and tenants to 50 percent tenants, 30 percent landlords, and 20 percent owner-cultivators. And, most relevant for our purposes, the compensation for the land taken from landlords (and the price to be paid by tenants for their new land) was calculated at 1945 prices and extended over thirty years, which, with inflation, quickly became ridiculously low. As one observer noted, one-quarter acre of good rice land that would have bought over 3,000 packs of cigarettes in 1939 was worth only 13 packs by 1948.[21] When conservatives objected to the amount of compensation, the Minister of Finance did not deny the economic insufficiency but countered that the legislation was not simply economic in aim but "drafted with the political purpose of effecting a change in the social structure."[22]

[20] Dore, *Land Reform*, 134.

[21] Ibid. 139.

[22] Finance Minister Ishibashi at Dore, *Land Reform*, 144.

Implementation

The Minister of Finance was correct. The change in social structure was profound and lasting. In 1941, over 53 percent of land was tenant-cultivated; by 1950 – still two years before the passage of the comprehensive Agricultural Land Law – it had fallen to 11 percent. The number of tenant households declined similarly so that only 5 percent of farm households were cultivating any rented land and only 5 percent owned no land at all.[23] The initial impetus for the legislation was pressure applied to the Cabinet and Diet by the Allies, but foreign pressure cannot explain the depth and consistency of the reform's implementation. Despite the dispossession of the landlords who owned more than half of Japanese agricultural land, there were only 110 violent incidents during the height of the reform in 1947–8. Nor was there slippage once the Americans left. Tenancy remains vanishingly rare today[24] and, as we will see, the idea of the farmer-owner has become virtually sacrosanct in Japanese politics, indeed to the point where most observers consider it a problem, not a virtue.

The credit for the implementation, therefore, must go substantially to the rural population and the degree to which they embraced the democratic premises and ideals of the land reform. Two excerpts from the minutes of the proceedings of village level Agricultural Committees illustrate this. The first concerns an owner who was trying to avoid being treated as an absentee landlord:

Committee Chairperson:	Are we to consider O as an absentee landlord or not?
Tenant Member B:	There is no evidence that he was living in the village in 1945 so he should be treated as absentee.
Tenant Member C:	We have gone on being swayed by "sympathy" and "human feeling" (*ninjō*) long enough. The matter should be settled according to the intentions of the law.
Landlord Member D:	C is right when he says that we should base ourselves on the law, but, when within the provisions of the law, the matter ought to be settled according to "human feeling."

[23] Table 8 from Dore, *Land Reform*, 175.

[24] Masayoshi Honma, *Gendai nihon nōgyō. no seisakukatei [The Policy Process in Modern Japanese Agriculture]* (Tokyo: Keio University Press, 2015), 82.

OWNER-CULTIVATOR MEMBER E: I understand what D means. But hitherto we have had too much feudalism in this village. Now we are having a land reform and if we are going to carry out thoroughly the intentions of the law I don't see how we can do what D suggests.[25]

The second excerpt concerns a landlord who was trying to terminate an existing tenancy and take direct control over his land. To do so, even at the end of the lease, now required his tenant's consent.

COMMITTEE SECRETARY: ... (A)n application by landlord L for permission to take back into his own cultivation land at present leased to tenant T. I have visited T and understand that he gave his consent because, as stated in the application, the original contract had expired and moreover his wife has been ill lately and he has not had the labor to farm the land properly.

TENANT MEMBER A: Whatever the reason might be on the surface, the fact is there is a long-standing connection between the landlord and the tenant, and the latter would hardly be in a position to say "no" to L if he wanted to. Look at the amount the two of them are cultivating at the moment and their respective financial situation. It is obvious that T needs the land more than L does. We ought to look at the facts of the situation.

CHAIRPERSON (TENANT): If what A says is true then I think we should go into the matter thoroughly and not give our approval simply because the tenant has given his formal consent.

[25] Dore, *Land Reform*, 158. It is worth noting that the idea of farmer-owners at the core of the land reform was shared by *nōhonshugi* and the prewar rightwing and that this ideological congruence may have contributed to the acceptance by conservative farmers of what was in many ways a radically leftwing policy.

TENANT MEMBER A: I suggest that we leave the matter over to the next meeting and meanwhile send somebody to find out more about the matter.[26]

At the next meeting, a *landlord* member reported that tenant T had been deeply indebted to landlord L and could not therefore refuse L's request. The committee then rejected L's application despite T's consent.

The Agricultural Land Law of 1952

The culmination of the land reform was the passage of the Agricultural Land Law.[27] Intended as the comprehensive codification of the previous legislation, many expected a conservative backlash, especially since the Occupation had ended and the Americans were now more concerned about Japan's reliability as an ally in the Cold War than about its democratization. But the ALL changed very little of substance. It kept the drastic limitations on landlord holdings and the broad definition of absentee landlords; most importantly, it put political goals at the forefront:

> *Article One* In recognition that the land ownership by farmers themselves is most important, the purpose of this law is to provide the security of the status for farmers and increase of the agricultural productivity by promoting the acquisition of the farms by farmers, protecting the rights of the farmers, and regulating the mutual utilization of farm land in order to ensure agriculturally productive use of land.

Productivity was explicitly not "most important" or the purpose of the law. To the extent that large-scale agricultural techniques were found to be desirable, they would be accomplished not by concentrated land holding but by "mutual utilization" of land among cooperating independent owner-farmers.

To ensure that Japanese farmers remained owners, the ALL severely restricted the market in land. Although not *de jure* prohibiting land sales as in the Tokugawa Era, the ALL was considerably more effective in practice. It brought all agricultural land transactions within the direct control of the local, prefectural, and central governments.[28] A detailed account of the provisions is unnecessary, but these principles are worth noting:

1. All transfers of agricultural land, including leases, required the permission of the Agricultural Committee.

[26] Dore, *Land Reform*, 157–8.
[27] Honma, *Policy Process*, 83, Owada, *Secret History*, 326, and Osawa, *Theory and Development*, 66.
[28] Honma, *Policy Process*, 84.

2. The transferee had to be capable of engaging in the cultivation of the land on a fulltime basis. Non-farmers who currently lacked such capacity were barred even if they wished to cultivate the land in the future.
3. Transferees had to be natural persons or an Agricultural Production Corporation (APC), the latter of which was limited to closely held entities for specific farm families.
4. Conversion of farm land to non-agricultural uses had to be approved by the prefectural governor or the Ministry of Agriculture Forestry and Fisheries (MAFF) (Article 4).[29]

These restrictions had the desired political effect. Cultivators were guaranteed – effectively required – to have the title to their land. The supposedly subservient tenants of the prewar period were replaced by individual proprietors fiercely jealous of their economic, social, and political status and their independence. The rural poor, who had recently seemed equally susceptible to the blandishments of the extreme left and right, became middle-class pillars of mainstream conservative politics and, enabled by an increasingly malapportioned Diet, the most reliable constituency of the Liberal Democratic Party, which has essentially governed Japan throughout its almost seven decades of postwar peace, prosperity, and freedom.

As we will shortly see, the restrictions on agricultural land that arguably contributed to these remarkable political successes eventually took an economic toll on Japan and even on farmers themselves, but at first the economic effect of the land reform was positive. Although there is debate as to whether productivity initially increased,[30] the economic and social status of tenant families certainly did. Some of that improvement was the result of protectionist policies that have harmed Japanese consumers and the competitiveness of Japanese agriculture, but these pernicious effects did not appear until the third decade of the reform, after the ALL's political goals had been fully achieved.

The Judicial Reaction

The low rate of violence notwithstanding, Japanese landlords were not happy. Although their success in limiting the scope of the initial legislation was stymied by the Americans, they continued to fight back politically through the 1950s and had many supporters in the conservative parties that dominated Japan. Unfortunately for them, however, the electoral math was not in their favor. When party leaders had to choose between a countryside made up of a

[29] Osawa, *Theory and Development*, 57.
[30] See Ramseyer, "Fable," 946–54, for the argument that productivity decreased immediately.

minority of supportive landlords and a majority of hostile tenants versus one made up of independent owner-farmers, they chose the latter. It is said, for example, that in the 1952 debate over the ALL, Finance Minister Ikeda Hayato of the conservative Liberal Party won over his party's reluctant members by arguing that the creation of a large number of satisfied owner-farmers by the land reform had "built the ideal *jiban* [political base] for a conservative party – and we have got to keep it." Another member, this one from the similarly conservative Democratic Party (the two parties soon combined to form the Liberal Democratic Party), pointed out that tenants outnumbered landlords and that creating more of the former would simply produce more voters for the Japan Communist Party.[31] By the end of the 1950s the political die had been cast and the Japanese landlord class had disappeared, replaced in their support of conservative politicians by their former tenants.

Democratic politics was not the only avenue of opposition, however. Despite its current reputation as a society disinclined to use law, Japan had been governed by a Western style legal system since the Meiji Restoration, prewar litigation rates were commensurate with those of other developed countries, and the courts had been effective vehicles for resisting government measures in the past.[32] Furthermore, the Meiji Constitution, which remained in force until it was superseded by the Constitution of Japan in 1947, protected the right of private property, as does its successor. It is not surprising, therefore, that landlords turned to litigation. By 1949, they had lodged close to 100,000 objections to the plans of local Agricultural Committees for the acquisition and redistribution of their land, had taken more than 25,000 appeals to prefectural Agricultural Committees, and had filed more than 4,000 lawsuits. A total of 119 of these suits argued that the land reform violated Article 29 of the 1947 Constitution, which states that "The right to own or to hold property is inviolable" and that the state may take private property by eminent domain only for a "public use" and only "upon just compensation therefor."

To the plaintiffs, transferring private land from one private party to a second private party did not constitute a "public use." The public use requirement comes directly from the US Constitution, and while no comparison of

[31] Dore, *Land Reform*, 422.

[32] Indeed, tenants used the courts successfully to resist the elimination of traditional leaseholds by the formalization of land law during the Meiji Period. See Kaneko, "New Trends." For more general discussion of Japanese attitudes toward litigation, see Frank K. Upham, "Weak Legal Consciousness as Invented Tradition," in *Mirror of Modernity: Invented Traditions of Modern Japan*, Stephen Vlastos ed., (Berkeley: University of California Press, 1998), 48–64. For an account of the postwar creation of low litigation rates, see John Owen Haley, "The Myth of the Reluctant Litigant," *Journal of Japanese Studies* 4 (1978): 359.

national doctrine can pronounce with authority on the propriety of a specific case, taking one person's title and giving it to another individual would almost certainly have been found to have violated the American Constitution at the time. It was not until the *Hawaii* v. *Midkiff* case in 1984 that the American Supreme Court allowed the forced transfer of land from one person to another.[33] Although the political and economic contexts are quite different, the basic facts of the two cases are strikingly similar. In both, the government took land from landlords and sold it to their tenants. In *Midkiff*, the transfer was aimed at eliminating a land tenure system that had only 22 families of former missionaries controlling 73 percent of the Oahu residential land market. The State of Hawaii argued that transferring title was necessary to eliminate an oligopolistic land market, and the US Supreme Court unanimously agreed.

What an American court might have decided in 1953, when the Japanese Supreme Court upheld the land reform by a 10–4 vote, we can't know, but doctrinal analysis is probably the wrong place to go in this context. The Hawaiian legislature was concerned with a malfunctioning land market; the Japanese Diet was just emerging from a devastating defeat and attempting peaceful social revolution, not the lessening of transaction costs. The better comparison might be the constitutionality of Lincoln's Emancipation Proclamation of 1862, which justified the taking of some slave-owners' property not as public use but as a measure necessary to win the Civil War. While the war was over for the Japanese government, Lincoln's situation seems closer to that of the Japanese Diet in the 1940s than that of the Hawaii legislature in the 1980s. Unfortunately for our speculative purposes, the constitutionality of the Emancipation Proclamation was never decided for the simple but conclusive reason that the Thirteenth Amendment to the US Constitution, passed in 1865, mooted the issue.

It is possible, therefore, that the "right" answer in terms of mid-century jurisprudence was that the land reform would not have constituted "public use," but this was the lesser of the government's constitutional issues. More difficult was the level of compensation. Japanese landlords received compensation calculated at 1945 prices on an estimated owner-cultivator's annual profit capitalized at current market rates of interest and expressed in terms of a fixed multiple of the official land value used for taxation purposes. An additional bonus payment based on rental values was available but limited to only a small amount of land. Significantly, only the bonus was in cash; the rest in the form of bonds redeemable after thirty years at 3.6 percent interest per annum.[34]

[33] 467 U.S. 229 (1984).

[34] Dore, *Land Reform*, 139.

At the time that the law was passed in 1946 inflation had already eroded the value to the point where it was worth approximately 50 percent of an average annual crop at the legal price and much less at the higher black-market price. By the time the money was paid, it was worth 10 percent of that figure – the thirteen packs of cigarettes.

If we revert to our American doctrinal comparison, the landlords' case looks very strong. In the USA, the measure of justice when it comes to the taking of property is simple: the fair market price, which the Japanese land reform measure would surely have failed, especially if the higher black-market prices for agricultural commodities were the measure. Nonetheless, the Japanese Supreme Court had little trouble with the case. On the level of compensation, the Court pointed out that under the second paragraph of Article 29 private property rights "shall be defined by law, in conformity with the public welfare" and that the price at which property could be compulsorily purchased was subject to the necessities of the public welfare. Indeed, the question had already been raised in relation to the Land Adjustment Act of 1938 and the series of war-time controls that had redefined rights in agricultural land in such a way as to "leave no room for a free market price of land to develop."[35] One of the minority opinions was a bit more straightforward, arguing that the land reform was the result of the supraconstitutional powers of the Allied Occupation and that the Supreme Court was powerless to do anything about it in 1953. Those judges, however, wanted to go on record that nothing similar could ever be done again.

It is clear that law was not the vehicle for the Japanese land reform in the same way that it was in the English enclosures and in the nineteenth-century America. There were simply too many other factors at play, most obviously a lost war and a military occupation determined to instigate a thoroughgoing land reform, but law was a necessary component, and the Japanese Supreme Court could not be taken for granted. The early 1950s were a time of significant judicial activism on behalf of the weak in Japan. In addition to validating the land reform, the Supreme Court substantially rewrote labor law, essentially converting an at-will employment regime to one in which it became extremely difficult to fire an employee, even for cause, and eliminated no-fault divorce in direct defiance of clear legislation providing for it. In both instances, the court referred to prevailing social norms, in the former the reciprocal loyalty of the employment relationship, in the latter the inherently moral basis of marriage. If either dismissals or divorce had been uncommon or considered inappropriate before these decisions, perhaps the court's reasoning

35 Ibid. 433.

could be taken at face value. In fact, however, before and after the war, divorce rates were high and employment protection weak, which was, of course, precisely why the court felt it necessary to rule as it did. The economic situation was dire and too many husbands were divorcing wives and marrying mistresses without any provision for the welfare of the former.[36]

While both of these decisions reversed clear legislative action, they both became seen by the public not as judicially imposed but as reflective of Japanese culture. If in the postwar period one asked Japanese why employers never fired incompetent workers or why the divorce rate was so low, the answer was invariably "Japanese culture." The Supreme Court decisions that mandated these practices were never mentioned. It is not farfetched, therefore, to imagine that the Supreme Court's approval of land redistribution and of the owner-cultivator principle of the land reform had a similar culture-forming role, if not in the counter-majoritarian sense of the employment and divorce decisions, then at least in affirming the legal, political, and moral propriety of the legislative destruction of landlords' property rights. In any case, the culture of the independent family farmer has dominated Japanese agriculture for well over half a century and it is to the economic cost of that structure that we now turn.

FROM POLITICAL EXPEDIENCY TO MARKET EFFICIENCY

Article One of the ALL was unambiguous in its statement of priorities. An agricultural sector of owner-cultivators was "most important" and the purpose of the law was to "provide security of status" for farmers. Agricultural productivity was a secondary goal, to be achieved solely through cooperation within the owner-cultivator class.[37] As we have seen, the ALL succeeded admirably in its primary goal. In this section, we examine the economic cost of that political success. Most striking is the impact on Japanese consumers, who pay among the highest food prices in the world, but the restrictions on the agricultural land market necessary to guarantee that Japanese farmers remain owner-cultivators have also distorted the agricultural sector in ways that damage the sector itself and the economy as a whole.

Viewed from any perspective except that of a conservative politician, Japanese agricultural policy today is a disaster. Even from the viewpoint of the farm population itself the situation is socially if not economically dire. Income is maintained by anticompetitive protectionism and subsidies, but

[36] Frank K. Upham, "Stealth Activism: Norm Formation by Japanese Courts," *Washington University Law Review* 88 (2011): 1493.

[37] Honma, *Policy Process*, 85.

the population is dwindling and aging.[38] Whole regions are depopulated with very few young people and with farms dominated by what is known as *sanchan nyōgyō*, or "three dears agriculture," the three dears being grandparents and their daughter-in-law. All the others have left for the more dynamic possibilities of the city. The stagnation is due not solely or perhaps even primarily to the lack of potential in Japanese agriculture – some sectors unconnected with government policy thrive[39] – but to a combination of restrictions on farmers' property rights and income protection and price subsidies that sustain the otherwise economically untenable status quo.

Many of the restrictions relate to the transfer of agricultural land. Most fundamental is the difficulty of converting agricultural land to any other use except sale to the government for infrastructure projects.[40] Japan wants to be self-sufficient in its basic food needs, so conversion to non-agricultural use, particularly of rice paddy land, is discouraged while rice cultivation is subsidized and rice imports restricted. The result has been rice surpluses as farmers produce for guaranteed prices in the face of weakening demand caused by decreasing population and changing diets. The underlying political motivation is a familiar one. As we will see in the next chapter, China also restricts the conversion of agricultural land for precisely the same reason, and the United States, while criticizing food self-sufficiency policies of its agricultural trading partners, restricts energy exports for fundamentally identical reasons.

Added to the concern for self-sufficiency is the political power of established agricultural groups, a pattern repeated in many societies with significant agricultural sectors and responsive political systems. Rice farmers, after all, are highly organized and cast ballots that are often weighted more heavily than those of their urban customers. Meanwhile, their potential replacements – farmers growing cutting-edge products desired in urban markets – are largely in the same position as the future residents of Sun City were in the *Bristor* litigation: they do not yet exist. Japanese consumers arguably bear the greatest cost, but two factors have prevented them from demanding effective reform. The first, the fact that their economic interests are diffuse, is common to consumers everywhere, but they are also unlikely to push for fundamental change

[38] See generally Yoshihisa Godo, *Sayonara nippon nōgyō [Goodbye Japanese Agriculture]* (Tokyo: NHK, 2010). For the aging of the population, see p. 106. For the general disappearance of rural population, see Young-Jun Lee, *Chihō shōmetsu: Tōkyō ikkyoku shūchū ga maneku jinkō kyūgen [The Disappearance of the Region: The Rapid Population Decline Brought on by Monopolar Concentration in Tokyo]* Hiroya Masuda ed., (Tokyo: Chuokoron-shinsha, 2014), 243.

[39] One example are those farmers who have adopted Dutch-style agricultural management and grown without government support. See Honma, *Policy Process*, 369.

[40] Ibid. 89.

because they too worry about food self-sufficiency and have deep, if often irrational, fears about the safety and quality of imported products, especially food.

But restrictions on conversion of agricultural land driven by fanciful fears of future food shortages should Argentine, Australian, and American producers collude to refuse to sell their beef, wheat, and rice to the Japanese are far from the whole story. Equally significant are the statutory principle of the owner-cultivator and an antipathy toward corporate agriculture that have driven agricultural policy since the passage of the ALL in 1952. Because of a fear of concentrated land ownership, even transferring land to other farmers for agricultural use is tightly restricted. Part of the problem is that owners are reluctant to lease excess land even to other individual farmers because regaining possession of leased land is difficult,[41] but the more general problem is the prohibition on selling to any entity other than an owner-cultivator or closely held Agricultural Production Corporation owned by an active owner-cultivator. As a result, fertile land lies fallow as the owners, no longer interested in or capable of farming, wait for the opportunity to sell once conversion becomes legally possible.[42] The rationale of all these restrictions, which remained more or less intact through the first decade of the twenty-first century, has been the preservation of the family farm, and the family farm has endured, if only in a distorted and attenuated form.

It is not that the decline of Japanese agriculture has gone unnoticed. Attempts have been made since the 1960s to make the sector more productive and competitive. In 1961, with the enactment of the Agricultural Basic Law, the Japanese government began to move away from a singular focus on the owner-cultivator principle by emphasizing the mechanization of larger farms. Then in 1970, Article One of the ALL was amended to add "for the purpose of efficient use of the farm land" to the preexisting promotion of "the mutual utilization of farm land," and the Ministry of Agriculture, Fisheries, and Forests began using the language "the principle of cultivator" instead of "the principle of farmer-owners."[43] The rest of Article One, including the language "land ownership by farmers themselves is most important, the purpose of this law is to provide the security of the status for farmers," remained, however, as did the elaborate process required for land transfer. The result was an incoherent co-existence of an emphasis on efficiency and larger-scale farming with the security and preservation of family farms. In practice, the latter prevailed virtually unchanged.

41 Godo, *Goodbye*, 106.
42 Ibid., and Honma, *Policy Process*, 180.
43 Yoshihisa Godo, *Nihon no shoku to nōgyō [Japanese Food and Agriculture]* (Tokyo: NTT Publishing, 2006), 157.

There followed a series of statutes and national agricultural plans that nibbled around the edges of the principle of owner-cultivator but stopped short of real change. Governmental rhetoric, both legislative and bureaucratic, began to stress food stability and the economic health of rural areas rather than farmer ownership, and in 2000 the Diet again amended the ALL to loosen the restrictions on the ability of Agricultural Production Corporations to own land and manage farms. None of these measures addressed the basic issue, however, and it was not until June 17, 2009, and the "Agricultural Reform in Heisei Era" that the Diet amended the ALL and other agricultural legislation to move significantly away from an emphasis on family farms and toward agricultural productivity.[44]

Even here, however, the reluctance to embrace the market fully was clear. The original bill submitted to the Diet by the Cabinet in 2009 was amended by three key additions, shown here in italics:

> In realization that agricultural land on which domestic agriculture is dependent is now and will be in the future a limited resource for the citizens *as well as a precious resource for certain regions, and based on the important role played by land ownership by farmers themselves,* the purpose of this law is to contribute to food stability for citizens by providing for increased agricultural productivity *and security of status for farmers* through restricting the conversion of agricultural land to non-agricultural use but also promoting the acquisition of title by productive farmers who use land in a regionally appropriate manner, *regulating the mutual utilization of agricultural land,* and taking measures to ensure the agricultural use of agricultural land.

The ambivalence is tangible. Driven by the Ministry of Agriculture Forestry and Fisheries' desire to increase agricultural production and reinvigorate rural Japan, the government wanted desperately to liberalize the sector. A majority in the Diet may have shared those goals but was constrained by the strong political support for the status quo. The result was a supposedly thoroughgoing "Heisei Era" reform of Japanese agricultural policy that has incorporated the very incoherence that has plagued the more incremental reforms of the past several decades. It is too soon to know whether the new stress on productivity and the other specific measures of the 2009 revision will be successful in changing the course of Japanese agriculture or simply another rearranging of the deck chairs on the Titanic. Nor is it certain that the failures of the contemporary policy arise directly out of the success of the original land reform in the first years of the postwar period. It is possible that the landlords, if left alone

[44] For a comprehensive discussion of the process, see *Juristo,* 1388.

to continue to dominate the countryside socially and economically, would have developed an equally powerful political class able to demand equally inefficient economic rents, as has arguably been the case in other developed democracies without a land reform of Japan's depth and scope.

What is clear, however, is that the elimination of the landlords' property rights in the late 1940s was hardly in vain. On the contrary, just as the enclosure of English commons and the polluting of the Meadow Brook allowed those societies to respond to market opportunities and create vast wealth, Japan's land reform helped create one of the world's most successful and stable democracies. It is of course possible that preserving landlords' economic, social, and political status might not have limited Japan's democratic development, just as preserving their property rights and allowing the land market to operate without restriction might have led to a woefully inefficient agricultural sector. Perhaps, in other words, a thoroughly democratic Japan did not require a rural sector dominated by family farmers. That is not what foreign and domestic political actors thought at the time, however, and the one thing that we can be sure of is that their policies achieved precisely the intended results.

In the next two chapters, we return to the destruction and recreation of property structures to take advantage of emerging market opportunities, first in late twentieth-century China, then in contemporary Cambodia, two societies that have responded in ways similar to those described in our previous case studies, but, significantly, without the legal institutions of early modern England, nineteenth-century America, or twentieth-century Japan.

5

Law and Development without the Law Part

China

We have examined the central impact that formal law can exert in shifting the legal right to valuable resources, whether for purely economic reasons (England, America) or for political as well as economic purposes (Japan). We now turn to the very different case of China, specifically its last four decades of explosive economic growth, an achievement in which law, in both legislative and judicial forms, has played little part.

To understand how China developed so quickly without the presumed basic legal necessities of economic growth, we look at four different areas of economic success: the township and village enterprises or TVEs, which thrived in rural China during the almost total legal vacuum of the 1970s and 1980s; the improvised structures created by foreign direct investors and their Chinese partners to substitute for formal property rights; the sometimes legal, often corrupt, and usually unfair expropriation of farmers' collective land by expanding cities; and the emergence of illegal but vibrant, sustained, and diffuse real-estate markets, known as "small property rights," in most large Chinese cites. But before we get to the stories of growth in these four sectors, some historical background is necessary.

THE EVOLUTION OF CHINESE PROPERTY LAW SINCE REFORM AND OPENING

Despite the primacy of the industrial proletariat in Marxist theory, the Chinese Communist Party (CCP) came to power in 1949 on the backs of poor tenant farmers and immediately rewarded them with a comprehensive land reform.[1]

[1] This description of the doctrinal evolution of Chinese property law is drawn from Chuanhui Wang, *The Constitutional Protection of Private Property in China: Historical Evolution and Comparative Research* (Cambridge: Cambridge University Press, 2016), 45–78.

The new regime's provisional Constitution had declared that the state "must systematically transform the feudal and semi-feudal land ownership system into a system of peasant land ownership," and a thoroughgoing redistribution of land followed immediately under the Land Reform Act of 1950. By 1953, 40 percent of Chinese land had been redistributed to 60 percent of the population, and almost 300 million farmers had received approximately 700 million *mu* (1 hectare = 15 *mu*) of agricultural land.

In 1954, the first Constitution of the PRC ratified the land reform and established four forms of ownership: state, individual worker, capitalist, and collective. The last encompassed rural land and foreshadowed the eventual elimination of individual land ownership. The collectivization process had begun in 1948 with voluntary Mutual Aid Teams, went through various forms of decreasingly voluntary cooperatives, and eventually culminated in 1958 in the transfer of all remaining private rights to local People's Communes of which all farmers became members. From 1958 to Deng Xiaoping's "reform and opening" of 1978 the People's Communes constituted the dominant *de facto* form of land ownership in rural China, but it was not until the Constitutions of 1975 and 1978 that law caught up with practice and the four ownership forms of the 1954 Constitution were legally reduced to the state and collective forms that constitute constitutional property today.

The commune system dramatically decreased agricultural productivity but continued until 1978 when Xiaogang, a poor village in Anhui Province, began leasing land to families for cultivation outside of the commune system. Although attempted by others earlier, this experiment, initiated with some trepidation by Xiaogang farmers,[2] succeeded spectacularly and was almost immediately adopted by the central government as the Household Responsibility System (HRS) in a 1980 Central Party declaration entitled Several Issues Concerning Strengthening and Improving the Agricultural Production Responsibility System.

Within a year of its promulgation, 98 percent of collectives had adopted the system and were contracting out land to individual families for periods that began as fifteen years, but that lengthened progressively; the present default period is thirty years with the full, if *de facto*, expectation of indefinite renewal. Security of tenure has strengthened along with duration. At first, villages commonly reallocated land to address changes in family size such as births, deaths, and the departure or return of a married or divorced daughter. By the end of the century, however, such reallocations were limited to natural disasters and similarly

[2] The eighteen leaders of the Xiaogang experiment were so worried about official reaction that they all executed wills in case of arrest. Wang, *Constitutional Protection*, 50.

extraordinary events, and households enjoyed in practice, if not law, indefinite tenure. As we shall see, however, even indefinite tenure falls importantly short of ownership, at least when one's land becomes attractive to those with power.

The jurisprudential distinction between *de facto* and *de jure* land use rights may have meant little to most farmers, especially at a time and in a context where there was a strong likelihood that a court would refuse to accept a politically controversial land case. The legal niceties of the evolution of the HRS system deserve our attention nonetheless because they illustrate the interaction between formal law and nonlegal policy that has characterized Chinese property law – indeed virtually all forms of law – throughout the history of the PRC. We must note, therefore, that not only did the Xiaogang experiment of 1978 have no legal basis, but the same might be said of the Central Committee's declaration two years later that immediately expanded Xiaogang's model to the entire nation. Not only was there no statute authorizing the policy change but the HRS directly contradicted Article 7 (2) of the 1978 Constitution, which stipulated that individual households could possess land only for residential and family use. It was not, in other words, only the Xiaogang villagers who were acting illegally but also the Central Committee. In China, however, such deviations from formal law are standard practice. If a new policy direction is successful, law can follow, as a brief review of the constitutional recognition of private property will illustrate.

The process began in 1988 with an amendment that allowed the transfer of land use rights "according to law" and for state protection of the "lawful rights and interests of the private sector of the economy." A more fundamental step came in 1993 with the recognition in Article 11 that the private sector constitutes "an important component of the socialist market economy" and the replacement of "socialist public ownership economy" by "socialist market economy." The change amounted to a belated but unequivocal declaration of China's turn away from central planning and to voluntary exchange premised on the decentralized control of economic assets, if not on a fully articulated version of private property.[3] The 1993 amendment also eliminated People's

3 See Minxin Pei, *China's Crony Capitalism: The Dynamics of Regime Decay* (Cambridge: Harvard University Press, 2016). Pei argues that the decentralization of control of state-owned property is a major cause of rampant corruption that he, and others, claim seriously threatens the survival of the current regime. See particularly pages 31–6 and 67–76. Pei made similar claims about the limitations of Chinese institutions in an earlier book, *China's Trapped Transition: The Limits of Developmental Autocracy* (Cambridge: Harvard University Press, 2006). For a similar analysis of China's potential stagnation with a particular focus on legal institutions, also from 2006, see Kenneth W. Dam, *The Law-Growth Nexus: The Rule of Law and Economic Development* (Washington, DC: Brookings Institution Press, 2006).

Communes and finally recognized the HRS inspired by Xiaogang fifteen years earlier. The year 2004 saw the most recent advance for private property under the Constitution. Article 13 now states that "Citizens' lawful private property is inviolable;" that "the State, in accordance with law, protects the rights of citizens to private property and to its inheritance;" and that the State may only expropriate private property in the "public interest and in accordance with law" and with compensation.

A superficial reading of this evolution of property norms would put the current constitutional status of private property on a par with that of the United States and Japan in that all three systems require both a public justification and adequate compensation for the state to acquire private property. While superficially accurate, such a reading would be seriously misleading. To begin with, Chinese courts are not effective guarantors of private property, both because of institutional incapacity and because official policy until recently had been to settle property disputes, especially social conflict over land, extra-judicially. But it would also be misleading to rely on constitutional norms because the Constitution and statutes evolve independently. The Constitution is not self-executing, and courts are not permitted to apply constitutional provisions directly in interpreting statutory law and deciding cases. Direct application must await the incorporation of constitutional norms by implementing statutes, which has often been slow in coming.

For observers accustomed to an integrated network of constitutional and statutory norms applicable to litigation, the system can be confusing. A recap of the evolution of the formal legal basis of the HRS may help. As we have seen, the contractual allocation of commune land to individual households began in one poor village in 1978. At that point, it was not only *ad hoc* and experimental but also directly contrary to the Constitution of 1978. Central Committee fiat then applied it nationally, and in 1982 a constitutional amendment acknowledged the general direction of economic reform. Four years later it was statutorily recognized for the first time with the passage of the Land Administration Law. The 1993 constitutional amendments completed the turn to the market at the constitutional level, but the terms of the HRS were not fully elaborated until the Rural Land Contracting Law of 2002, which provides for thirty-year renewable terms for arable land, thirty- to fifty-year terms for grazing land, and thirty- to seventy-year terms for forest land.

Urban land has followed a distinct but parallel path.[4] Private use rights in urban land were effectively eliminated in the 1950s by the collectivization

[4] See Shitong Qiao, "The Politics of Chinese Land: Partial Reform, Vested Interests, and Small Property," *Columbia Journal of Asian Law* 29 (2015): 70, and Eva Pils, "Contending

movement, then formally nationalized by the 1982 Constitution, only to be gradually relegitimated since. The process has been much more straightforward and gone much further toward total liberalization than has been the case with rural land. The near-total dependence of city residents on either their local government or state-owned employer for housing began to be dismantled in 1979 on an experimental scale and "housing commercialization" became national policy when transfers "according to law" were constitutionally recognized in the 1988 amendments. The process continued in 1994 with the passage of the Law on Urban Real Estate Administration, which provides two methods to acquire land use rights from local governments. One is government allocation, primarily used for land to be put to public use. The other is leasing, which is the main way that individuals and enterprises acquire land use rights. For residential use, the maximum term is seventy years, for industrial use fifty years, and for commercial use forty years. The result is an urban land market that resembles in practice, if not legal form, similar markets where allodial land ownership is the norm.[5]

The most recent significant step in the evolution of statutory, as opposed to constitutional, property law was the passage in 2007 of the Property Law by the National People's Congress. Despite the ambitious title, the legislation did not change much. Although it did clarify such matters as whether owners of ground-floor condominium units must contribute to elevator maintenance or whether the developer or homeowner association owns the parking spaces in residential subdivisions, it left most of the pressing issues untouched. The reason for the reticence was simple: Land has become one of the greatest sources of social conflict in contemporary China and is arguably the most controversial and most fundamental legal and policy issue facing the government and Party today.[6] The Property Law's recognition that private property enjoyed the same protected status as public property was already intensely contentious. To go further and decide unresolved fundamental questions such as the correct measure for compensation for farmland or the path to legalization for illegally

Conceptions of Ownership in Urbanising China," in *Resolving Land Disputes in East Asia: Exploring the Limits of Law*, Hualing Fu and John Gillespie (eds.) (Cambridge: Cambridge University Press, 2014), 115–72.

5 Donald Clarke, "China's Stealth Urban Land Revolution," *American Journal of Comparative Law* 62 (2014).

6 For one representative example of social protest, see Owen Guo, "A Chinese Farmer's Execution Shows the Pitfalls of Rapid Urbanization," *New York Times*, November 16, 2016. For a discussion of the controversy surrounding the Property Law, see Frank K. Upham, "From Demsetz to Deng: Speculations on the Implications of Chinese Growth for Law and Development Theory," *NYU Journal of International Law and Politics* 41 (2009): 551.

possessed land threatened to delay the law's passage indefinitely, and, as we have seen, the national legislature is emphatically not where legal decisions are initially made, but where they are ratified after they have already been implemented as national policy.

THE ABSENCE OF PROPERTY RIGHTS IN CHINESE ECONOMIC GROWTH

If China did not possess legally defined property rights enforceable in the courts, some other social processes enabled economic actors, whether they were Chinese farmers or multinational corporations, to "form those expectations which he can reasonably hold in his dealings with others." Although a full description of what those processes were is beyond the scope of this chapter, a quick tour of four sociolegal phenomena can provide an overview, but first a clarifying definitional note.

No "Law" at All?

Even a summary account of the role of property in China's transition from a planned economy and collectivist society to a market economy and consumer society raises three questions about the role of institutions in society. First is the preliminary question of what constitutes law in contemporary developing countries. The second is a function of the first: what social structures played the role conventionally attributed to law in China's growth and could similar institutions play that role in other poor countries? The third and most fundamental question asks what conclusions we should draw from three decades of rapid economic growth without legislated legal norms enforced by an independent and effective judiciary.

As the reader will have noted, policies and practices precede law in contemporary China. The communes were instituted despite the 1954 Constitution's provisions for private ownership of farmland. They were not legally authorized until the 1975 and 1978 constitutions, which were almost immediately violated by the introduction of the HRS. The HRS was not legalized until the 1982 Constitution and not fully articulated in statute until the 2002 Rural Land Contracting Law. The process of normative change has been similar for the liberalization of urban land use rights, and we can expect any future legal reformulation of rural land use rights to follow a similar pattern of regional bureaucratic experimentation, national adoption of successful measures through executive policy announcements, and statutory ratification only well after full implementation.

Only *falü* – statutes passed by the National People's Congress – qualify as law in China. In this sense, much of government action is lawless: there is either no law governing specific conduct or the relevant law is ignored. This does not mean, however, that official governance is informal in the sense that it is arbitrary and, in Shihata's terms, left "to the whims of the ruling individual or clique." Nor is it informal in the romantic sense of reflecting a traditional customary order or community consensus. China's transitions from private ownership of land to collectivization and then part of the way back may not have been legal in our narrow usage, but they were officially initiated by political leadership and proceeded in response to rules, just not formal rules passed by a constitutionally empowered legislature. It may not have been *law*, but it was *order* and a far cry from the lack of centralized normative order that occurs in many developing countries, particularly in relation to land.[7]

The consistent maintenance of public order raises the question of whether we should take such a positivist approach when discussing China's changing property law or whether we should instead identify the order created by the administrative system as law. My conclusion is that the strict usage is necessary both in examining China and to understand the role of law, by any definition, in development more generally. The PRC itself recognizes the distinction between the bureaucratic order I have described and the legal order of National People's Congress legislation. Indeed, the October, 2014, Fourth Plenum of the Central Committee of the Communist Party emphasized, *inter alia*, the development of China's formal legal system, including the strengthening of the judiciary, a clear indication that the leadership not only sees the difference between bureaucratic order and formal law, but also that it recognizes the value of the latter.[8] That said, as we see in the next four sections, China's "lawlessness" usually includes a degree of order and stability that can effectively play the role typically attributed to a robust legal system.

Ownership Rights in TVEs

Township and village enterprises (TVEs) were the "growth engine" of reform in China until the 1990s and Exhibit A in most commentators' discussion

7 Daniel Fitzpatrick, "Evolution and Chaos in Property Rights Systems: The Third World Tragedy of Contested Access," *Yale Law Journal* 115 (2006): 996.

8 For an overview of the contradictory relationship between China's efforts to create *fazhi*, commonly translated as rule of law, and its insistence that courts and government operate under the control of the Communist Party, see Jerome A. Cohen, "Law's Relation to Political Power in China: The Domestic Situation" (forthcoming publication of the Herbert Ma Foundation, Taipei, Taiwan).

of China's ambiguous property rights.[9] They varied greatly in structure and operation, but their defining commonality was collective ownership by the residents of the village or township in which they were located. Ownership was in name only, however, as TVEs were controlled by local government and Party leaders, who in turn delegated day-to-day operation to managers. Local officials were in turn accountable to their superiors in the state apparatus, not to the local residents who were the legal owners. The presence of this agency slack did not mean, however, that the owner-residents did not benefit. Most employees were residents, and most revenues went toward the provision of public goods such as schools, transportation, and infrastructure. The community, or "mass autonomous organization" according to the Chinese Constitution, was not in legal control, however, either through some form of shareholding or elections.

De jure ownership, in other words, was virtually irrelevant, at least in the commonly used sense of defining and enforcing rights. The ephemeral nature of formal law is powerfully described in Chih-jou Jay Chen's study of property rights in two villages with dramatically different economic and political structures.[10] Shuang Village in Jiangsu Province was dominated throughout the reform period by Communist Party cadres. Hancun Village in Fujian Province, by contrast, was dominated by preliberation family firms that consistently resisted effective state control. In Shuang, even the eventual privatization of TVEs was contained within the circle of local officials while the most that the local government in Hancun could achieve was forcing the private firms to "wear a red cap," i.e., to accept rhetorically collective ownership, and pay tribute to the township treasury.

In both villages property rights were ambiguous and judicially unenforceable, and yet both enjoyed spectacular growth. Although the state played a role that was at times parasitic – corruption and rent-seeking were rampant – it did not do what many economists argue every state will do if not prevented by formal property rights: It did not steal all the wealth of successful businesses.

9 For an overview see Barry Naughton, *The Chinese Economy: Traditions and Growth* (Cambridge: MIT Press, 2007). Naughton calls TVEs the "'motor' for the entire transition process" at page 3. For evaluation by other China scholars, see, e.g., David L. Wank, "Producing Property Rights: Strategies, Networks, and Efficiency in China's Nonstate Firms," in *Property Rights and Economic Reform in China*, Jean C. Oi and Andrew G. Walder (eds.) (Palo Alto, CA: Stanford University Press, 1999): 248.

10 Chih-jou Jay Chen, *Transforming Rural China: How Local Institutions Shape Property Rights in China* (London and New York: Routledge Curzon, 2004). For a discussion of the formal and informal institutions that provided structure for the TVEs and later destruction of that structure, see Teemu Ruskola, "People, Inc.? Law, Economic Enterprise, and the Development of Inequality in China," *American Journal of Comparative Law*, forthcoming.

Officials' restraint may well have been motivated by personal ties to the community, but their opportunism was also limited by political and social structures – not legal ones – that made it undesirable, difficult, and unnecessary for the state to kill the golden goose that was doing so well for the local economy, the local society, and ultimately the local government and party bureaucrats themselves.

The TVE story is important but there are many reasons to doubt the broader applicability of any "model" that might be gleaned from it. For one thing, the successes of Shuang and Hancun were highly contingent on local circumstances, making generalization difficult. For another, TVEs thrived in the earliest days of reform before large-scale legal construction (however one might define law, there was little of it at the time) and during the initial primitive stage of China's transition to markets. They were small, local, and oriented toward taking advantage of immediate market opportunities and lacked the long-term perspective required for sustained market success. Indeed, most TVEs have now been at least partially privatized, and the economic form is no longer a prime driver of the economy.

One might be tempted, therefore, to dismiss the TVEs' apparent contradiction of conventional wisdom as an idiosyncratic response to economic and legal anarchy relevant only to very poor countries at the earliest stages of economic growth and with little to say about how to get beyond the immediate goal of alleviating desperate poverty in the rural hinterlands. Since desperate poverty persists in much of the world, dismissal of the TVE story on this ground would be a serious mistake, but it would also be a mistake because the phenomenon of ambiguous property rights has not disappeared as China has gone from least-developed to middle-income status. On the contrary, it has persisted, as we can see by looking at the role of property law in foreign direct investment (FDI).

Foreign Direct Investment

China is now the world's leading recipient of FDI, meaning that non-PRC individuals and businesses have poured vast amounts of money into China without the close personal ties and geographical proximity that undoubtedly contributed to the security of TVE investments. That they have done so without formal legal institutions provides further evidence that the conventional wisdom that formal property law is indispensable for arm's length, large-scale, sustained commercial transactions is at least incomplete if not simply wrong.

Recent work on Chinese FDI by Weitseng Chen demonstrates that "substitutes established by foreign investors for formal property institutions fulfill various functions that are otherwise supplied by a state-backed property regime."[11] Foreign investors use these institutional substitutes to provide three fundamental attributes of property law: security of tenure, alienability, and dispute resolution. These are delivered through a range of jury-rigged legal and nonlegal, formal and informal structures that defy easy summary but offer another example of the alternatives to developmental orthodoxy.

Although Chen notes the existence of informal practices such as hiring local officials for no-show jobs and relying on reputational networks, he stresses the innovative use of legal forms such as corporate structure and contract to provide substitutes for property rights institutions and an effective judiciary. Some of these workarounds are illegal, such as the "subcontracting manufacturing factories" that allow foreign firms to "unlawfully lease land ... and begin their export-oriented manufacturing."[12] Others, such as joint ventures [JVs], are legal but instead of being used for their intended purposes have been employed to accomplish ends normally achieved through formal arrangements and functioning courts. As Chen puts it, "Without a functional judiciary to enforce various contracts, foreign investors may reduce legal risks by transforming numerous business deals into internal business decisions of a JV company."[13]

The FDI story demonstrates that formal legal institutions, if not property law institutions per se, have not been absent in Chinese growth. The use of contracts and the joint venture form to substitute for effective property rights shows that formal law and imaginative lawyering were relevant to protecting

[11] Weitseng Chen, "Arbitrage for Property Rights: How Foreign Investors Create Substitutes for Property Institutions in China," *Washington International Law Journal* 24 (2015): 47. The investors investigated by Chen are largely overseas Chinese, which raises the possibility that it is shared culture and language that enable commercial transactions without the standard legal institutions. He argues, however, that such culturally created trust is intertwined with and cannot exist without institutions and, further, gently implies that to discuss trust in the Chinese context alone suffers from a tinge of Orientalism: "A rational American is unlikely to trust a British stranger and set up a business with her simply because they both speak English and know who William Shakespeare is. It is unlikely that those who share a common Chinese culture are any different." Chen argues that because some of his "institutional substitutes" are based on formal legal institutions such as contracts and corporate form, China does not "overrule the orthodox view" about "the indispensable role of property rights in economic growth." Chen, "Arbitrage." Since he amply documents not only the innovative nature of the use of formal law in these practices but also its frequent illegality and at times criminality, I believe that his assertion that the orthodox view remains unscathed can be true only if we take the orthodoxy as the original broad approaches of Demsetz and North, i.e., that institutions and hence in this context "law" include informal norms.

[12] Chen, "Arbitrage," 61. These contracts with local governments were illegal at least until the late 1980s. See Chen, "Arbitrage," 59.

[13] Ibid. 67.

investment even if their function has been far from that anticipated by their drafters. Before we discuss whether and how this use of law factors into the broader questions of this book, however, we examine two instances where law and its absence have affected ownership and use of land, which remains the most broadly important form of property in contemporary China. In one, the annexation of rural farmland by expanding cities, formal institutions have been employed to their intended end, although not consistently or faithfully. In the other, the "small property rights" real estate market, vibrant markets exist in direct defiance of formal law.

The Transfer of Agricultural Land to Urban Use

China is in the midst of an urbanization process of unparalleled scale. Hundreds of millions of new residents have entered Chinese cities since 1980 and hundreds of millions more are likely to do so over the next few decades. To accommodate these new residents, large areas of rural land must be converted to urban use, which might be simply and quickly done if a functioning legal market in land use rights existed, but it does not. On the contrary, the transfer of rural land use rights for urban use is prohibited. As we saw above, farm land is collectively owned by village residents in a way similar to TVEs and is legally limited to agricultural use. For it to be used for urban purposes, it must first be formally expropriated by the local municipality and converted to state-owned urban land, after which the city can sell use rights at market prices.

Expropriation must satisfy certain legal criteria. It must be in the public interest; those affected must be consulted; and compensation must be paid.[14] The requirements of public interest and consultation are similar to American and Japanese doctrine, but the measure of compensation throughout most of this period departed substantially from practice elsewhere, from law and development orthodoxy, and from basic principles of economic efficiency. First, it was unclear who should receive the compensation, the collective that owns the land or the individual member households who own the rights to use it. The law seemed to choose the former and rely on the collective to ensure that individual households were in turn compensated. Second, the compensation award was largely based on the discounted value of the usufruct right for agricultural use. Since the duration of that right went from fifteen to thirty

[14] For an outline of legal requirements for expropriation, see Lei Chen, "Legal and Institutional Analysis of Land Expropriation in China," in *Resolving Land Disputes in East Asia: Exploring the Limits of Law*, Hualing Fu and John Gillespie (eds.) (Cambridge: Cambridge University Press, 2014), 59.

years during this period, the amount increased similarly from the value of fifteen years of crops to thirty.

The missing element in the process, of course, is the total disconnect from market value. Since rural land could not be legally sold for non-agricultural use, there was no existing legal market, but had sales been legal, a market would have immediately developed and produced a price close to that which the local government received when it sold the land to developers. In fact, there was and is precisely such a market, but it remains illegal as we will see in the next section, and expropriation remains the only legal way to transfer land to urban use. The effect has been to guarantee that urban governments get farmers' collective land at a small fraction of its market value.

The weaknesses of this legal framework from a micro-economic perspective are substantial, the most important being the lack of voluntary exchange coupled with a failure to pay anything close to production value for taken land. But actual practice was often much worse and was enabled by the inaction of the courts.[15] No one will be surprised to learn that local village officials colluded with municipal officials and real estate developers, that the required consultations with collective residents did not always take place, that the full prorata share of compensation did not always make it to the dispossessed households, that urban employment and housing promised to farmers to persuade them to agree to annexation often did not materialize, and that money went missing on a massive scale. It is impossible to state with confidence how often irregularities occurred – indeed in many areas along the prosperous eastern coast, farmers have become rich[16] – but land disputes were often cited as the primary cause of social conflict.

What is important for our purposes, however, is that the courts generally opted out of these disputes. They simply would not accept the cases; other times, they forced mediation on the parties; and at other times they diverted

[15] The role of courts has evolved over the forty years in question. For an account of a relatively early dispute where the courts simply refused to intervene, see Eva Pils, "Land Disputes, Rights Assertion, and Social Unrest in China: A Case from Sichuan," *Columbia Journal of Asian Law* 19 (2005): 244. For accounts of the more varied recent approaches, see Xin He, "Administrative Law as a Mechanism for Political Control in China," in *Constitutionalism and Judicial Power in China*, Stephanie Balme and Michael W. Dowdle (eds.) (New York: Palgrave Macmillan, 2009), and Jie Cheng, "The Judicial Role in Land-taking Cases," in *Resolving Land Disputes in East Asia: Exploring the Limits of Law*, Hualing Fu and John Gillespie (eds.) (Cambridge: Cambridge University Press, 2014), 86.

[16] And not only rich, but happy. I once asked a former farmer, now a driver for university academics and a shareholder in collectively owned apartment buildings constructed with compensation from land expropriation, if he missed farming. He smiled and responded, "You've never been a farmer, have you?"

the grievances from the intended defendants to less politically sensitive targets.[17] The reason was simple: The cases were too politically charged for local courts to intervene against local governments. Some observers condemn this passivity as a dereliction of the courts' most important role; others consider it a cautious and pragmatic strategy that preserves the limited power and autonomy that courts currently enjoy.

We do not have to make that judgment. For our purposes, all that matters is that no one was enforcing property rights and yet China grew faster than any other significant economy in the world. Would China have grown even faster if property rights were enforced? It seems unlikely. Indeed, the wholesale destruction of property rights may have made the transfer of valuable factors of production from agricultural to urban uses quicker than either the scrupulous adherence to expropriation procedure or even voluntary exchange had the PRC granted individual farmers alienable property rights and allowed them to negotiate arm's length sales to willing buyers. All the political, social, and economic factors that delay, raise the cost of, and sometimes prevent altogether such transfers in rule-of-law capitalist economies simply were not an issue. From the foreign investor's point of view, as Weitseng Chen put it, "a one-party Leninist regime ... may reduce the transaction cost tremendously."[18] Does this ease of process mean that ignoring property rights was a good thing? Of course not. It simply means that property rights were not necessary for economic growth. If we want to justify property rights, at least in contemporary China, we must find a non-economic rationale for doing so.

Small Property: Vibrant Land Markets without Rights

The rigidity of Chinese land law, specifically the legal inability of collective owners to use land non-agriculturally, has spawned a second phenomenon that is less politically prominent but that poses a more complicated question

[17] Cheng, "Judicial Role," 106, cites a 2003 "Circular Regarding Cases Courts Should Not Accept" from the Guangxi High Court ordering provincial courts to refuse to accept, *inter alia*, land cases "because they are complex, vexatious, and costly" and "lead to enforcement difficulties." Susan Whiting and Shao Hua describe the use of mediation to deflect and defuse conflict, "Courts and Political Stability: Mediating Rural Land Disputes," in *Resolving Land Disputes in East Asia: Exploring the Limits of Law*, Hualing Fu and John Gillespie (eds.) (Cambridge: Cambridge University Press, 2014), 222. Xin He describes how courts deflect already-controversial cases into safer channels, "Protest-supported Housing Demolition Litigation and Social Change in China," in *Resolving Land Disputes in East Asia: Exploring the Limits of Law*, Hualing Fu and John Gillespie (eds.) (Cambridge: Cambridge University Press, 2014), 194.

[18] Chen, "Arbitrage," 73.

for reformers than abusive expropriation: the illegal development of rural land on a massive scale. Known as "small property rights" to denote their inferior nature in comparison to fully legal "big property rights," this form of informality is ironically caused not by expropriation, but by the failure of cities to expropriate enough. Because of the social and political issues discussed above and because China, like Japan, limits conversion of agricultural land in the name of national food self-sufficiency, expanding cities have not taken enough land quickly enough to come close to meeting the demand. The result has been the emergence of broad and deep illegal markets in virtually all major Chinese cities. We will use Shenzhen to illustrate the scope of that market.[19]

Situated immediately north of Hong Kong, Shenzhen is the country's fourth largest city and the symbolic heart of the Chinese economic miracle. It is also the city with the largest and most dynamic illegal market in real estate and the highest ratio of small-property buildings: 48 percent of its total floor space, compared to 30 percent in Xi'An and 20 percent in Beijing. These illegal buildings are spread across 320 intra-city "villages" whose land is still legally classified as rural despite being in the middle of a city of over ten million inhabitants. Small property residences host most of the eight million migrant workers in Shenzhen and are the main source of income for the more than 300,000 original villagers. It is important to note, however, that they are not characterized by the low-quality construction evoked by the stereotype of informal housing in the developing world but include modern buildings of high quality.

This market has resulted from the huge gap between the land's agricultural value and its value when used, even illegally, for other purposes. It is sustained

[19] This account of Shenzhen's small property rights market is based on Shitong Qiao, *Chinese Small Property: The Co-Evolution Of Law and Social Norms* (Cambridge, UK: Cambridge University Press, 2017). Small property rights in Shenzhen is very much a community phenomenon with the village administrations playing a central coordinating role, but small property rights can be an individual phenomenon as well, and in those individual cases, courts have been willing to respond. A quick review of one 2007 case from the Beijing Second Intermediate Court (#13692) will illustrate not only how the market developed but also its legal nature. The case began in 2002 when Li Yulan, a Beijing artist, purchased a house in the suburban "painters' village" of Songzhuang from farmer Ma Haitao. Village authorities recognized the sale and Li later applied for and received official permission to renovate the house. The deal went sour in 2006 when Ma realized that land values in Songzhuang were appreciating rapidly and that there was a chance of formal annexation of the area by Beijing, which would mean a large compensation award. Ma accordingly demanded the house back and, when Li refused, sued for its return on the basis that the original contract was void because it was in direct violation of the law. The court agreed, vacated the sale, and awarded ownership to Ma, but required Ma to compensate Li for the renovations and increases in the market value of the house.

by the changing economic, political, social, and legal relations among village residents, government agencies, and real estate developers. A market network has grown from participants with strong ties to each other to those with weaker ties, and eventually to participants with no preexisting relationship whatsoever. In other words, China's small property market, like its market for foreign investment, extends outwards from bounded communities to unbounded parties, including foreign investors, and all without a framework of judicially enforceable legal rules.

The property arrangements that individuals or groups can make are determined by their specific positions within the social network of the village and are dependent on their status as original residents of the rural collective. What allows a market of close-knit parties to open to strangers, however, is the direct involvement of professionals like lawyers and real estate brokers, commercial institutions like banks, and even different levels of the local government. The scope and vigor of this market not only challenge the orthodox view that only official institutions implementing legal rules can create the lasting security necessary to sustained economic growth, but also pose a challenge for Chinese leaders: how eventually to integrate small property into the legal system.

Their options can be portrayed on a spectrum. At one end would be the vindication of the law whereby all illegally constructed buildings would be demolished and their developers punished. The sheer scale of the market all but precludes this option. Although informality does not dominate China's urban landscape as it does some Latin American and African cities, 20 percent of Beijing, 30 percent of Xi'an, 45 percent of Shenzhen, and similar numbers across China would mean a lot of demolition, resettlement, and punishment. But the problem is not solely one of scale. The network of relationships that sustains small property markets goes way beyond the individual squatters and shady real estate developers that one associates with informal housing in poor countries. Brokers advertise the properties and bring the parties together. Lawyers certify that the resulting transaction has been entered into voluntarily by both parties and retain copies of relevant documents for subsequent review by later buyers or lessees. Local state-owned banks provide individual mortgages for ordinary buyers and large-scale financing for industrial parks, commercial malls, and high-rise apartment buildings built by foreign investors. Small property, in other words, is not a departure from the Shenzhen real estate market, but a core part of it on which large segments of the professional and middle class depend and in which many participate.

A last but important reason to doubt the possibility of simply repudiating small property rights is the complex and contradictory role of government. Chinese municipalities are divided into three levels, city, district, and sub-district, and illegal buildings have different implications for each level. The city and district governments are generally hostile to small property. They are responsible for aggregate economic development and prefer big investors to small ones, and land is often the key asset that the city has to offer large investors. The more land is occupied by small-property shops and restaurants, the less it is available to attract large-scale newcomers.

The sub-district governments, on the other hand, are directly involved in accommodating millions of migrant workers and in governing the day-to-day life of the entire population. For agencies with specific missions such as health, safety, or sanitation, close cooperation with small property owners is essential. For example, the Bureau of Business Administration grants business licenses to enterprises (restaurants, factories, shops, etc.) located in small-property buildings on the condition that the village collective certifies that the buildings are appropriately rented or owned by the enterprises; similarly, the Municipal Office of Housing Renting (MOHR), which is one of the agencies with responsibility for public security and social stability, registers and assigns identification numbers to all small-property buildings in its system and cooperates with village collectives in the taxation and the management of the migrant population. As a MOHR official said: "[W]e knew these buildings were illegal. Our registration has nothing to do with illegality; we just want to maintain social stability by closely monitoring the migrant population, most of whom live in these buildings."[20] In what must be the ultimate symbol of accommodation, some sub-district offices are located in small-property buildings.

THE CHINESE EXPERIENCE AND PROPERTY LAW THEORY

When we return from the Chinese case to the general themes of this book, we are faced with two related questions: whether the various roles that formal law has played and not played in the last four decades of Chinese development require us to rethink the assumptions of property theory and, second, whether we can learn enough from the Chinese experience to guide us as we consider whether and how contemporary poor societies should use formal property law to emulate Chinese economic growth. Put more simply, does China prove the current orthodoxy wrong and should there be a China model for the poor world to emulate?

[20] Shitong Qiao interview with a government official, July 1, 2012.

Is the Theory Wrong?

To answer this question, we must initially return to the founders of neo-institutional economics. If we take what they wrote rather than how their ideas have been implemented, the answer is quite possibly no. China created a bureaucratic and social order that supported investment and sustained markets without the formal property rights that contemporary law and development practitioners proclaim to be necessary, but Demsetz and North did not claim that economic assets had to be protected by formal norms. Under the varying rubrics of customs, mores, mental models, and ideologies, they explicitly anticipated that informal norms could play the roles reserved for courts, legislatures, and lawyers by today's rule of law reformers. And this insight has been advanced by others. Michael Trebilcock, for example, described similar informal structures in the radically different context of Papua New Guinea over thirty years ago.[21]

It does not immediately follow, however, that the normative structures that provided order during China's growth are consistent with the informal norms foreseen by Demsetz and North. They, too, might be surprised that a Marxist-Leninist one-party state could create an institutional framework that could vindicate so emphatically their theories of the roles of property rights and market exchange. From an objective perspective, however, the Chinese experience seems entirely consistent with the fundamental message of both scholars. Demsetz's Montagne Indians were neither liberal democrats nor endowed with a separation-of-powers bureaucracy. Nor did North claim that the particular allocation of political power that animates Scalia's law of rules was uniquely appropriate for economic growth.

Happily, we don't have to settle these issues, but only whether Chinese growth undermines the standard prescription that mandates creating or reforming the institutions of poor countries' legal systems according to templates derived from formalist Western models. Here, the answer seems to be yes, although there is evidence that China's formal legal institutions have at times played a significant role in managing social conflict. Xin He[22] and Benjamin Liebman[23] have described how judges have left their chambers and

[21] Michael J. Trebilcock, "Communal Property Rights: The Papua New Guinean Experience," *University of Toronto Law Journal* 34 (1984): 377.

[22] Xin He and Yang Su, "Street as Courtroom: State Accommodation of Labor Protests in South China," *Law & Society Review* 44 (2010): 157.

[23] Benjamin L. Liebman, "Malpractice Mobs: Medical Dispute Resolution in China," *Columbia Law Review* 113 (2013). Columbia University Academic Commons, http://dx.doi.org/10.7916/D8445M3B.

turned the streets into courtrooms to settle labor and other contentious disputes when populist anger threatens social harmony. But both authors stress the social and political, not the legal, role of the judiciary. Indeed, their point was the deviance from the letter of the law, not its vindication. Similarly, it was the rhetorical red hat of collective ownership worn by Hancun merchants that secured their interests, not the law, which would have repudiated the private ownership that their red hats protected. The story is the same with small property rights: legal institutions are involved but outside of the formal framework. The lawyers facilitating the deals, after all, are doing so not only in direct defiance of law but also of the orders of the Guangdong Province bar association. Even in Weitseng Chen's description of the use of contracts and corporate structure in FDI, the forms and doctrines are found in unusual places performing unanticipated functions normally reserved for property law.

So, even where legal institutions were involved, they played roles far from that expected by the orthodoxy, and in many instances, such as the TVEs, they were simply absent. Furthermore, most of the evolution of property law over these decades, with the HRS most prominent, occurred without any statutory basis and often in direct contradiction to existing formal norms. Equally striking has been the general absence of courts from controversial cases. Courts have been involved in many small property rights disputes among individuals, but when property has been threatened by important social or government actors, the courts have looked the other way. And yet the economic interests of foreign and domestic investors in China have not been so violated that growth has stopped. Quite the contrary, and in that sense it seems impossible to deny the importance of the Chinese experience in reevaluating the current dogma.

Before declaring law irrelevant to economic growth, however, we must consider whether the Chinese economy has reached a stage where a law-of-rules type of legal system is necessary to advance beyond its current level as a middle-income country. And in terms of development broadly defined we must also consider whether the political consequences of China's current property system threaten regime stability.

Has China's Order without Law Reached an Impasse?

Kenneth W. Dam's 2006 *The Law-Growth Nexus: The Rule of Law and Economic Development* is a rare and able instance of the law and development orthodoxy responding seriously to the phenomenon of China.[24] As the title

[24] Dam, *The Law-Growth Nexus*. See Upham, "From Demsetz to Deng," 564–76, for an analysis of the lack of impact of Chinese economic growth on law and development theory. Where

indicates, the book is a general explication of the role of law in growth, but unlike most such works, Dam's does not ignore China. He tackles its recent history directly and in depth, recognizing that growth has occurred without much in the way of property or contract rights and concluding his book with a chapter entitled "China as a Test Case." That alone would make the book worth examining, but it is also worth examining briefly because his conclusion represents the popular view that China may have done alright without law up to the present, but is likely to crash if it does not create an effective legal system quickly.

Dam's recognition that China has grown rapidly without law is important, but he doesn't take the next step to conclude that we should reconsider the conventional wisdom at least as it relates to the poorest of developing countries. Instead of urging the study of Chinese substitute institutions, he emphasizes China's efforts to build a legal system as it has grown economically – what he refers to as the "filling in the chinks and gaps in the legal infrastructure" – and concludes that not too much should be made of China's story:

> It is certainly too early to accept the notion that recent Chinese experience is a counterexample to the need for a focus on institutions in the developing world and, indeed, for a rule of law in China itself. Rather the Chinese experience is consistent with [the] view that considerable development is possible without strong legal institutions but sustainable growth to higher per capita levels requires considerable development of legal institutions.

economists have dealt with Chinese economic growth without property rights, it has often been to find reasons to dismiss its general relevance. Ronald Coase and Ning Wang, for example, affirmed the orthodoxy, "It is not the case that the experience of market transformation [in China] challenges secure and well defined property rights as a legal foundation in the working of a market economy." *How China Became Capitalist* (New York: Palgrave Macmillan. 2013) 142, 173. The authors admit that the lack of TVE property rights was "rather peculiar," but attribute their success to their hard budget constraint and concluded that the focus on property rights in discussing TVEs was "misplaced." They did not speculate whether a hard budget constraint can always or generally substitute for the foundational role that they claim for property law. Consistent with his belief in history, politics, and culture, Douglass North was more willing to acknowledge the importance of China's accomplishments:

> The Chinese so far have not created the institutions of the western world; but they have created similar kinds of incentive structures with the household responsibility system and township and village enterprises (TVEs). Given their own background and cultural heritage, they have created these with their own kinds of rules and laws. And so far the system is working. The reason I say so far is that they have a long way to go. But one does not have to imitate western institutions and cultures.

The Role of Institutions in Economic Development, Gunnar Myrdal lecture, UN Economic Commission for Europe, Geneva, Switzerland, Discussion Paper Series No. 2003. October 2, 2003 www.unece.org/fileadmin/DAM/oes/disc_papers/ECE_DP_2003-2.pdf.

> While a definitive conclusion will not be able to be drawn for several decades, it is nonetheless clear that little thus far in the Chinese experience leads to the conclusion that rule of law issues are not important in economic development.

Dam is correct that nothing in the Chinese experience is inconsistent with the view that idealized rule-of-law institutions are required to reach high levels of per capita wealth. It is equally correct that the Chinese experience is consistent with the opposite proposition. The Asian financial crisis of the late 1990s has often been cited as evidence that high-flying Asian economies can only go so high before their defective legal systems bring them crashing down. It is certainly true that Thai, South Korean, Indonesian, and other fast-growing Asian countries' legal and regulatory institutions failed to prevent or contain that crisis, and some countries subsequently initiated significant legal reforms. It is equally true, however, that the legal and regulatory institutions of the United States failed to prevent the almost total collapse of Western financial systems in 2008. Indeed, it is plausible that the complexity and sophistication of American financial institutions contributed to a crisis that caused economic and social losses that eventually made the Asian financial crisis look like a mere bump in the road. These American institutions are, of course, precisely the models that Dam and others urged China to replicate so that it could eventually emerge as a fully developed economy. Chinese leaders must be pleased that they spurned this advice.

Is the Issue Politics, not Economics?

But further economic growth is not the only property law issue facing China. There is politics as well, and not only in the aspirational terms of Sen's human capabilities but also in the more immediate terms of institutional decay facilitated – if not created – by weak property rights.

Minxin Pei argues in *China's Crony Capitalism* that the very survival of Communist Party rule is threatened by collusive corruption enabled by poorly articulated lines of control over state property. As a political scientist, Pei's concerns are not as directly responsive to issues of law and development as are Dam's and raise a range of issues that go beyond even a broad review of property's role in development. Because his claim that the current regime is in decay is based on an analysis of China's legal system, however, it, too, is worthy of our attention. For Pei the doctrinal evolution described in the first section of this chapter was not only disconnected to the facts on the ground, but also fatally incomplete in "that partial and incremental reforms of the property rights associated with nominally state-owned assets in the post-Tiananmen era have decentralized control of these assets without clarifying their real ownership."[25] This ambiguity required cooperation among elites to "avoid mutual vetoes"[26] that would lead, in turn, to widespread, interlocking networks of corruption that defy prevention, detection, and prosecution.

The essential problem is not ownership per se, but a lack of clear lines of control exacerbated by the state remaining the nominal owner of much of the economy. The political, fiscal, and bureaucratic decentralization of the 1990s made the lines of control of state assets so vague and fragmented, both vertically and horizontally, that it created a new type of political corruption that required interaction and trust among a wide range of officials at different levels and across distinct administrative hierarchies. He acknowledges that a system of "mutual vetoes" might operate as a check rather than an accelerant to corruption in a different context and that the geographical and social cohesion of TVEs in the early days of reform may have had that effect despite the ambiguity of control.[27] Such has not been the case more recently, however, perhaps in part because so much of the target of corrupt officials has been rural land and real estate, ownership of which may be clearly in the collective but control of which is deeply ambiguous in precisely Pei's sense. It is worth noting in this context that Xi Jinping has singled out land in his current anti-corruption campaign.[28]

In sum, celebration of full development without property rights may not be in order quite yet from either the economic or political perspective. If the People's Republic of China collapses in the near future, we will have at least one clear answer. If it continues but growth stagnates, we may have another. It is simply too early to be certain about the final destination, but one observation seems irrefutable even for skeptics like Dam and doomsayers like Pei: China demonstrates beyond doubt that substantial economic growth and dramatic reductions in poverty are possible for desperately poor countries without such institutions. We now turn to whether that experience can provide some guidance for similarly poor countries or whether it is limited to complicating our faith in sacred cows.

[25] Pei, *Crony Capitalism*, 24.

[26] Ibid. 27.

[27] Indeed, scholars have argued that the looseness of the property rights system on the local level was conducive to growth despite its obvious inefficiencies. Wank, "Producing Property Rights," 248–72.

[28] "We must concentrate our crackdown on corruption in critical sectors such as mining resources, land transfers, and real estate development." Xi Jinping, January 23, 2104. Cited in Pei, *Crony Capitalism*, 23.

Is There a Chinese Model?

To claim a Chinese model or "Beijing Consensus," as some have done,[29] is much more difficult than critiquing existing doctrine. One must be able to create a positive story of the role of property institutions in Chinese development. By that I mean that one would have to identify which social structures created which informal norms that substituted for the role of legal rights in the orthodox model. It is not enough to assert that the Chinese experience disproves or weakens the orthodoxy. One must have a substitute explanation based on the Chinese experience, and that is just the first step. After one has determined with sufficient clarity and generality what provided security for investment and exchange in China, one must demonstrate that this new set of social and political institutions can be replicated elsewhere. Such, after all, has been the role of every nostrum embraced by the Western reformers from Rostow's stages of growth to the Washington Consensus. Even if "one size fits all" is no longer politically correct, the core idea of a model of sufficient generality to fit Bolivia, Burundi, and Bangladesh with a modicum of adjustments must remain. If not, there is neither a model nor a consensus. The point bears repeating. The idea that a model must fit "Bolivia, Burundi, and Bangladesh" is not alliterative hyperbole. What is required for a model or a set of "global best practices" is a template that can be applied universally with a degree of specificity that can guide concrete action in widely differing poor countries.

With China, I believe that even the first step of explaining its growth with clarity, generality, and precision will be very difficult, and the idea of applying it, even with adjustments, elsewhere seems extremely problematic. Indeed, even replicating it in some hypothetical rerun of the last thirty-five years seems unlikely. The variety of institutions and contexts that made growth possible without law is unlikely to be recreated even inside China, much less in other poor countries, each one of which has its own unique characteristics. Of course, people will try. One possibility is to broaden the perspective and claim that the model is some meta-characteristic of contemporary China. The usual suspects are Confucian culture or the Communist Party, but it is hard to call this approach either a model or a consensus. The point of both is to provide the basis for a course of action, and contemplating the creation of either Confucian culture or the CCP in other developing countries stops the conversation.

[29] For discussion, see Weitseng Chen (ed.), *The Beijing Consensus? How China Has Changed the Western Ideas of Law and Economic Development* (Cambridge: Cambridge University Press, 2016).

The failure to relocate the Washington Consensus to Beijing does not mean that we cannot generalize, however. Even if China's last three decades demonstrate that property rights are not necessary for economic growth, one might still draw some links connecting the legal nature of the Chinese experience and that of other countries that have grown rapidly. One is the tendency for countries to look for legal order even when growth has been achieved under conditions of illegality or a-legality. The examples are legion but we have already examined three: the English enclosures, the transformation of American water law, and the Japanese land reform. In each, property rights were destroyed for the sake of economic and political development. But in each instance, after the fruits of the destruction of property were harvested – economic growth and democracy, respectively – there was a rebuilding of property rights.

If we look hard, we may be able to discern a similar process in the examples of this chapter. Although more data are necessary, one might say that informality, illegality, and ad hoc institutional innovation have been followed by a movement towards formality, including legal formality. Such has been the case with the urban real-estate market and the privatization of the TVEs. The Supreme People's Court has also ordered local courts to accept land cases, although it is unclear whether this will occur in the service of social harmony ("street as courtroom") or formal adjudication true to the legal rules. In other words, what we may be seeing is the role of property rights in the political development of China, as opposed to its economic growth.

6

Theory in Action

Cambodia

In studying the relevance of contemporary property theory to developing countries we have seen three examples of the strong presence of formal law – economically driven in England and America, politically driven in Japan – and a powerful example of its absence in China. In this chapter, we examine the post-Khmer Rouge reconstruction of Cambodian property rights, specifically the 2001 Land Law, where formal law again plays the central role, but with a significant difference: courts remain in the background and legislation plays the key function in destroying and recreating property rights.

Because of its official status as one of the World Bank's least developed countries and its extreme dependence on the international community for technical, administrative, and financial support, Cambodian legal reform embodies development practitioners' aspirations for property law to a degree unusual even in small poor countries. The Law was initiated, drafted, and financed by foreign experts determined to create a legal regime that would put into practice the wisdom of neo-institutional economics as interpreted and applied by the World Bank and an alphabet soup – the ADB, CIDA, JICA, DANIDA, and GIZ – of other international aid agencies. Because the law is as close as one is likely to get to a pure application of social science theory to practice, an examination of its creation and implementation can further deepen our understanding – and elucidate the complexity – of the role of property rights in development. Specifically, it will allow us to assess the extent to which a system that offers clear, transparent, and conclusive title to land can deliver on its promises of growth and development.

Cambodia provides this opportunity because unlike the English, American, and Chinese examples, the transformation of its property rights regime was neither the product of domestic political forces nor a spontaneous, incremental response by market players to economic forces. Instead, like the Japanese land reform, it was an intentional decision by outsiders to improve the law, although in this instance with the primary goal of accelerating economic growth rather than creating democracy. In contrast to postwar Japan, however, where domestic political forces quickly captured the process, Cambodia's successive waves of foreign experts remained in control. They not only designed the relevant statutes but also funded and oversaw the building of the bureaucracies charged with their implementation. Nor did the foreigners have to worry about conflict with existing law. The Khmer Rouge had eliminated virtually all legal professionals and destroyed all records, leaving a clean slate as far as formal institutions were concerned.

This dependence on international organizations has one further benefit for our purposes: the whole process of legal reform has been closely watched. The multitude of international NGOs and publicly accountable aid organizations has meant that the Hun Sen government has not been able to prevent the open evaluation of policy. Indeed, the presence of institutions like the World Bank has led to recurring investigations of policy effectiveness by the Bank itself and by many of its critics. While each organization has its biases, the diversity of viewpoints provides data on a scale and depth rare in poor countries. If one is looking to study the role of property theory in development, it would be hard to find a better setting than contemporary Cambodia.

The chapter begins with an overview of Cambodian land legislation from the fall of the Khmer Rouge in 1979 with a particular focus on the foreign origin of the law and the influence of contemporary property theory. It then offers two case studies, one urban and one rural, of the operation of the new regime, and concludes with an analysis of the role of titling under Cambodia's 2001 Land Law. As we will see, law reform driven by best-practices development theory may be contributing to aggregate economic growth by, *inter alia*, providing clear property rights to large-scale investors, but at the cost of destroying the preexisting and statutorily recognized property rights of the relatively poor and powerless.

THE EVOLUTION OF CAMBODIA'S LAND LAW

Until French colonialization in the late nineteenth century, land in Cambodia was the property of the king but individuals had the right to possess, use, and pass land to their heirs so long as they continued to cultivate it.[1] When Cambodia became a French protectorate, individual rights to land that had

[1] For general treatments of Cambodian land law, *see* Sovann Sar, *Land Reform in Cambodia* (May 2002), and East West Management Institute, *Land Law of Cambodia: A Study and Research Manual* (Phnom Penh: EWMI, 2003).

been cleared and used were recognized by royal proclamation, but the concept of fully private title to land in the European sense was first introduced by the Civil Code of February 25, 1920. By 1930, most rice-growing land was registered as private property, but lack of bureaucratic capacity meant that only 10 percent of landowners received ownership titles, with the rest receiving certificates of possession.[2] This system of land administration remained largely unchanged through independence in 1953 and up to the Khmer Rouge takeover in 1975.

The Khmer Rouge abolished all private property and destroyed all records of ownership. The state owned all land and allocated it for use by "solidarity groups" in a massive socialist experiment. The experiment failed. As many as two million people died during the Khmer Rouge's five years in power, and annual rice production declined by almost 80 percent.[3] These material costs were exacerbated by the elimination of almost all educated people so that by the time the Vietnamese invaded in 1979 and established the People's Republic of Kampuchea (PRK) with Hun Sen at its head, there remained fewer than ten lawyers and fifty doctors and virtually no one with the legal, bureaucratic, or technical capacity to administer a cadastral system. The system of land management did not change significantly under the PRK. Land continued to be owned by the state and used by solidarity groups. Families were allowed small plots but there was no effort to restore private ownership, much less restore pre-1975 ownership rights.

Creating the Statutory Framework

With the departure of the Vietnamese, the renunciation of Marxist/Leninist ideology, and the creation of the United Nations Transitional Authority in Cambodia (UNTAC) in 1991, the establishment of a legal framework appropriate for a market-oriented democratic state began. UNTAC's Land Law of 1992 was a preliminary first step, but real reform began with the drafting of the 2001 Land Law. It was initiated, designed, and originally implemented almost exclusively by foreigners. A succession of European and World Bank cadastral experts drafted the law; then the bank-financed and -staffed Land Management Administration Project (LMAP) guided its implementation until 2009 when the Bank withdrew after an Inspection Panel discovered widespread

2 Sokbunthoeun So, "Land Rights in Cambodia: How Neopatrimonial Politics Restricts Land Policy Reform," *Pacific Affairs* 84 (2011):289, 291.

3 See United States Department of Agriculture, Foreign Agriculture Service, Commodity Intelligence Report, "Cambodia: Future Growth Rate of Rice Production Uncertain," January 26, 2010. www.pecad.fas.usda.gov/highlights/2010/01/cambodia/.

mismanagement and corruption. Although diluted by the Japanese-drafted 2007 Civil Code,[4] the Land Law introduced an Australian-based system that determines ownership exclusively on the basis of formal registration with a centralized cadastral agency. It guarantees transparency by refusing legal status to any informal use or possession of land and by providing for distribution of state land – the Cambodian state formally owns up to 80 percent of the country – only through grants directly from the central government.

To integrate Cambodia into the world economy,[5] clarity and transparency were considered of paramount importance. Accordingly, the law disavows any attempt to reestablish pre-1975 property rights and allows people who can demonstrate five years of lawful, good-faith possession of land as of 2001 to apply for "definitive title of ownership." Titling is neither automatic nor guaranteed, however. The claimant has to apply and affirmatively "prove that he himself fulfills the conditions of peaceful, uncontested possession for no less than five years."[6] If the possessor does not apply or is unable to satisfy the requirements, the land is considered to belong to the state, against which no

4 A full explication of Cambodian land law would require an examination of the doctrinal interaction of the Civil Code and the Land Law and the corresponding bureaucratic rivalry between promoters of the code, the judiciary and Ministry of Justice, and supporters of the Land Law, the Cadastral Commission and the Ministry of Land Management, Urban Planning, and Construction. For a discussion of the Japanese approach, see Yuka Kaneko, "An Alternative Way of Harmonizing Ownership with Customary Rights: Japanese Approach to Cambodian Land Reform." *Journal of International Cooperation Studies* 18:2 (2010): 1–21.

5 One government official noted that "We need land deals to attract foreign direct investment, provide employment, technology and human capacity, and infrastructure development, and as a way to properly manage national resources for the benefit of all Cambodians." Alison Elizabeth Schneider, "What shall we do without our land? Land Grabs and Resistance in Rural Cambodia," paper presented at the International Conference on Global Land Grabbing, Institute of Development Studies, University of Sussex, April, 6–8, 2011.

6 Article 30 states that,

> Any person who, for no less than five years prior to the promulgation of this law, enjoyed peaceful, uncontested possession of immovable property that can lawfully be privately possessed, has the right to request a definitive title of ownership. Any person who possessed the immovable property for less than five years may request a definitive title of ownership after five years of possession. In case the granting of a definitive title to ownership is subject to an opposition, the claimant has to prove that he himself fulfills the conditions of peaceful, uncontested possession for no less than five years over the contested immovable property or to prove that he purchased the immovable property from the original possessor or his legal beneficiary or from the person to whom the ownership was transferred, or from their successors.

Article 38 further requires that "possession shall be unambiguous, non-violent, notorious to the public, continuous and in good faith." The Inspection Panel, *Investigation Report Cambodia: Land Management and Administration Project* (Credit No. 3650 – KH) (Report Number 58016), World Bank, November 23, 2010, paragraph 64.

prescriptive possession can be recognized.[7] Unlike under the common law, where peaceable possession creates a rebuttable presumption of a right to continued possession, if the untitled occupant, whether a farmer or urban resident, cannot prove ownership, the state is deemed the owner. As we shall see, the default ownership of land by the state has had important consequences for large-scale land grants, but perhaps even more important for a poor country like Cambodia is what the law emphatically did not allow: No matter how long, open, and peaceful, post-2001 informal possession or use cannot ripen into ownership or even a continued right to possession.[8]

On the contrary, instead of relying on the facts on the ground, the drafters looked to Australia's Torrens system and created a regime in which title is determined exclusively by a cadastral registry to be established under the Ministry of Land Management, Urban Planning, and Construction [Land Ministry]. Three features deserve emphasis: registration is the sole path to ownership;[9] rightful owners defeated by fraud or mistake will be compensated by the state, but will not recover ownership;[10] and, crucially important in the developing world context, transfer is effective only if in "the authentic form drawn up by the competent authority and registered with the Cadastral Registry."[11] It was at this point and in order to "reduce poverty, promote social stability, and stimulate economic development" that the World Bank created and funded LMAP to supply the technical expertise necessary to begin the

[7] Article 43.

> In no case can the public property of the State be the subject of acquisition of ownership. The situation of an occupant of State public property remains precarious and illegal if such occupation was not authorized in the manner determined by this law. An illegal occupant shall be forced to vacate the premises immediately and shall be punished in accordance with Article 259 of this law. An illegal occupant is not entitled to any indemnity for any works and improvements carried out on the immovable property.

Unless otherwise specified all statutory texts come from the English version of the 2001 Land Law prepared by the MLMUPC Cambodia, supported by ADB TA 3577 and LMAP TA GTZ.

[8] Article 29. "Any beginning of occupation for possession shall cease when this law comes into effect."

[9] Article 239. "A cadastral index map and Land Register have legal value and precise effect."

[10] Article 226. "Ownership of immovable property shall be guaranteed by the State."

[11] Article 65. "The transfer of ownership can be enforceable as against third parties only if the contract of sale of immovable property is made in writing in the authentic form drawn up by the competent authority and registered with the Cadastral Registry Unit. The contract of sale itself is not a sufficient legal requirement for the transfer of the ownership of the subject matter."

quick, clear, and conclusive specification of ownership, commune by commune, throughout all of Cambodia.[12]

Registration comes in two forms: systematic and sporadic. The former is conducted by cadastral teams in preselected areas and provides separate titles to all residents; the latter responds to individual applications and targets only the applicant's land. From an aggregate perspective, the results have been impressive. As of 2010 the Cadastral Administration had issued more than two million title certificates, most of which are in rural areas and the product of systematic, rather than sporadic registration. More surprising, especially since the formal fees have been kept low, the process has been self-financing since the 2009 withdrawal of World Bank funding.[13]

Unfortunately, the aggregate statistics mask important shortcomings. An initial issue was the choice of which land should be the first to be systematically titled. LMAP's strategy was to begin with areas that were neither "likely to be disputed" nor of "unclear status" and to avoid "informal" settlements altogether. The rationale was to build administrative capacity and legitimacy through early successes.[14] Because "likely to be disputed," "unclear status," and "informal" were undefined, local authorities had essentially unfettered power to remove land from the cadastral process by placing it in one of these exempt categories. And because individually initiated sporadic registration is too costly for poor households to manage,[15] areas left out of systematic land

[12] World Bank, *LMAP Project Appraisal Document* 2 http://documents.worldbank.org/curated/en/643811468770346842/Cambodia-Land-Management-and-Administration-Project (January 2002). The Project was to begin with eleven selected provinces. See, Thomas J. Miceli et al, "Title Systems and Land Values," *Journal of Law & Economics* 45 (2002) 565 for the correlation of higher values with registration systems.

[13] The systematic titling process has collected data on 2,053,062 parcels, 80 percent of which are rural, and issued 1,500,493 title certificates. An additional 607,784 titles have been distributed through the sporadic process, bringing the total to 2,108,277. Cambodian Council of Land Policy, *Report on Achievements of Land Reform Implementation (2002–2009) and Ways Forward through the Program Based Approach (2009–2013)* 4 (June 2011).

[14] World Bank, *Statement from the World Bank on Termination by Royal Government of Cambodia of the Land Management and Administration Project*, available at: http://web.worldbank.org/WBSITE/EXTERNAL/COUNTRIES/EASTASIAPACIFICEXT/CAMBODIAEXTN/0,,contentMDK:22303344~menuPK:293861~pagePK:1497618~piPK:217954~theSitePK:293856,00.html. See Mark Grimsditch and Nick Henderson, *Untitled: Tenure Insecurity and Inequality in the Cambodia Land Sector*, 9 (2009) www.academia.edu/8476467/Untitled_Tenure_Insecurity_and_Inequality_in_the_Cambodian_Land_Sector. As informal settlements had no definition, in practice authorities often label urban poor communities as informal settlements, regardless of whether they have legal possessory rights under the law.

[15] Although formal fees are reasonable, informal "fees" and the need to hire a broker to manage the process make the total cost much higher. Estimates for sporadic registration of a "small piece of land" were $600–$800. Another source estimated that sporadic registration

registration have remained in a state of legal ambiguity. Therefore, while the owners of titled parcels have benefited both in terms of perceived security and enhanced access to credit,[16] these have been exclusively in areas where land is of low market value. As the World Bank eventually concluded, titling has been effective only where land is cheap and disputes rare. But where land is valuable and attracts "predatory interest" the program has been at best ineffective and at times destructive of tenure security.[17]

A second issue arises even in areas that have been systematically registered. Most Cambodians believe that holding the title certificate, as opposed to registration with the Cadastral Registry, constitutes ownership, which leads people to transfer land relying on the sale contract and certificate alone without registration. This pattern is neither new nor unique to Cambodia; it has been pervasive in similar titling programs globally.[18] As a French government White Paper recognized for titling programs throughout the developing world, "the laboriously created [registries] are often inoperable because they [are] rarely updated," meaning that it is often "only a few years before the discrepancy between the actual and the documented situation becomes a new source of insecurity."[19]

Accuracy is further eroded by bureaucratic practice and fraud. Local land officials routinely rely on documents rather than onsite investigation, which

---

cost $2,500. Sources agreed that informal fees also vary based on size and location and thus roughly track land value.

16 A 2005–6 survey of 1,236 households in titled areas found that 83 percent of those who had received titles felt "more content to have received them and felt securer." World Bank, *Inspection Panel Report*, paragraph 248.

17 See World Bank, *Inspection Panel Report*, paragraph 294.

18 *See*, e.g., Angelique Haugerud, "Land Tenure and Agrarian Change in Kenya," *Africa* 59 (1989) ("Nowhere has the Kenyan state had the capacity to keep the land registers up to date since the reform.") and Thomas C. Pinckney and Peter Kimuyu, "Land Tenure Reform in East Africa: Good, Bad or Unimportant?" *Journal of African Economies* 3 (1994): 1, 22–4 ("Formal changes of title are lengthy and expensive ... Title holding therefore does not necessarily imply ownership, and a significant number of titles are held by persons not owning the land ... Thus land titling in Kenya has in many ways caused more problems than it has resolved. One response of local communities has been to ignore the titles, and revert to the indigenous system of land tenure.") Kenya is a particularly well documented instance, but the pattern is pervasive. *See* generally the White Paper issued by the Agence Française de Développement [French Development Agency], *Land Governance and Security of Tenure in Developing Countries* (2009) (www.agter.asso.fr/IMG/pdf/land-governance-and-security-of-tenure-in-developing-countries.pdf).

19 French Development Agency, 61. The French White Paper severely criticized the "narrow technical approach to land tenure ... of Northern development agencies," which, it claims, fails to recognize the complexity of rural land practices in poor countries. In a statement that calls into doubt the long-term effectiveness of LMAP, it concludes that, "Land management is not going to be improved by superimposing land registries onto faulty legal systems."

means that an individual with falsified documents can dispossess farmers who have peacefully possessed the land and perhaps even registered it under previous regimes.[20] Greater community knowledge of the law and the need for registering subsequent transfers may help with some of these issues, but the experience of other poor countries and the failure of the Cambodian government to increase popular awareness of registration requirements do not provide assurance of long-term success.

Perfection should not be the metric, however, and shortcomings notwithstanding, registration has had notably positive effects. There is evidence that systematic titling has improved access to credit, as most banks will accept a registration certificate as collateral for a mortgage or other loan,[21] and certificates have proven useful in local disputes between community members of relatively equal status.[22] Moreover, the cost per title of Cambodia's systematic registration system, at least before "informal fees" are included, is among the lowest in the world. Nonetheless, the scale of the task is daunting. The total number of land parcels in Cambodia is estimated at upwards of ten million. At the current rate, to title the entire country will take decades even if the registering of lands "likely to be disputed" does not require any more time or resources than those titled up to the present.

Since the state formally owns 80 percent of Cambodia's land, however, registration of preexisting private ownership could never be more than a part of the answer to the population's land needs. One approach would have been to formalize the possession and use of post-2001 informal occupants, but it was feared that doing so would sacrifice the clarity of the registration system. Instead, the law preserved the transparency and conclusiveness of the registry by establishing a dual system of Economic and Social Land Concessions to transfer large parcels of state land directly to investors and the landless poor, respectively.

Both of these concessions are limited to state *private* land. The Land Law divided state-owned territory into two categories. State *public* land comprises both ordinary land devoted to public use, such as infrastructure, and land with an inherently public nature, such as nature reserves or cultural heritage sites. State private land is a residual category and is available for land concessions.

20 Interview by Gabriele Wadlig, summer 2016, with villagers involved in land dispute and Legal Aid lawyer in O'voi Preng.

21 Interview by Gabriele Wadlig, summer 2016, with private real estate lawyer and former World Bank consultant.

22 Interview by Gabriele Wadlig, summer 2016, with country director of international NGO. Note the similarity with Chinese courts, which can be effective in low-stake individual disputes, but generally ineffective when powerful interests are involved.

State public land is not available for distribution to private parties unless first converted to state private land. Unfortunately, the criteria for each category and the mechanism of conversion are unclear and the mandated mapping, categorization, and registration of state land in a publicly accessible database have not occurred, adding further uncertainty to the whole process. In some instances, the appropriateness of changing classification may be clear – a discontinued airport or a closed public school – but as we will see, there are many situations that are less obvious and where the lack of clear criteria and bureaucratic transparency can contribute to corruption and fraud.

Seeing Like an International Law Reformer

It is not just the doctrinal specifics that are crucial to understanding land reform in Cambodia, but the unprecedented influence and control exerted by foreign experts on the law's creation and implementation. The magnitude of what the World Bank, along with a host of aid agencies, and Western governments, including the United States, Japan, Germany, and Denmark set out to create in one very poor country is breathtaking. It exemplifies what James Scott has called "seeing like a state,"[23] i.e., top-down bureaucratic mapping of society in pursuit of specific government goals, in this instance the dual goals of providing clear title to foreign investors and ending landlessness. Scott's case studies included Stalin's collectivization of agriculture, Mao's creation of people's communes, and Nyerere's "villagisation" project in Tanzania. As with the 2001 Land Law, each of these aimed at creating an orderly, transparent, and rational rural sector out of what was seen by the reformers as premodern disorder and ideological backwardness.

What makes Cambodia's example remarkable, however, is that it was designed by foreign experts with reference to global best practices and with virtually no knowledge of or attention to the subject society. Whatever can be said of Stalin, Mao, and Nyerere, they knew their respective societies. The drafters of the Land Law, by contrast, did not even pretend to reflect or connect to prevailing social practice beyond the recognition of pre-2001 possession.

There are other differences. The animating ideologies, for one. Stalin, Mao, and Nyerere were intent not only on replacing capitalist or precapitalist

[23] James Scott, *Seeing Like a State: How Certain Schemes to Improve the Human Condition Have Failed* (New Haven and London: Yale University Press, 1998). It is also remarkably similar to the legal aspect of colonialization. The French Development Agency White Paper noted the similarity and described the colonial process as "creating private property from the top down" and ignoring the "previous rights of occupancy" in order to guarantee "indisputable" land rights to colonists. French Development Agency, 24.

structures of production with collectivist ones but also on replacing bourgeois attitudes with socialist ones. Most of today's development institutions have no *explicit* ideological goals;[24] indeed most international institutions are legally barred from politically motivated projects. Upon closer inspection, however, a consistent ideology emerges. At the level of LMAP and the Land Law, that ideology is the idealized version of neo-institutional economics described in Chapter 2 and the concomitant faith that clear legal title will facilitate Coasian bargaining and contribute to economic growth and development.

On one level, this ideology could not be more different from Scott's socialist examples. Instead of communal economic structures and collective action, ownership is privatized and action is individualized. Government goes from being an active shaper of society and direct participant in the economy to being a referee, and in societies like the United States, where the legal system is often considered distinct from the government, the state fades even further into the background. Land law and more general legal reforms become vehicles to emancipate individuals to operate in the market in ways that appear as the antithesis of government mapping. They aim to minimize, not maximize, government power.

To base policy on the assumption that the state can be relegated to the role of traffic cop, however, mistakes an ideological goal for attainable policy. It ignores Demsetz's warning of the nirvana world that too often tempts economists, but, even more ironically, it ignores the brutal fact of the massive government role in creating and maintaining a neo-liberal world. In rich societies like Australia, much of this work has been accomplished through centuries of bureaucratic and political trial and error but in least-developed countries like Cambodia, that foundation must be built from scratch – and it must be built immediately.

To free each Cambodian to act in her own self-interest, in other words, the state must first map, in this instance literally as well as figuratively, the entire country, and then assign each parcel to a specific individual. Thereafter,

[24] One exception is the United States, which unapologetically and explicitly aims at internal political change in foreign countries through, for example, the Democracy, Rule of Law, and Labor [DRL] program of the State Department. See United States State Department Bureau of Democracy, Human Rights, and Labor, DRL Programs, Human Rights and Democracy Fund:

> Often politically sensitive, HRDF [Human Rights and Democracy Fund] programs have a dramatic effect on democracy promotion and personal liberties. The programs enable the U.S. to minimize human rights abuses, support democracy activists worldwide, open political space in struggling or nascent democracies and authoritarian regimes, and bring positive transnational change. Sometimes DRL's HRDF programming is the only US assistance available to citizens fighting to change their societies.

www.state.gov/j/drl/p/index.htm Accessed December 2, 2016.

regardless of whether the mapping and assignments are accurate, it must impose, by force when necessary, the resulting network of newly created legal rights and obligations on all persons, including denying access to land to those who the local community may believe have superior moral, customary, or social claims to use, possess, or own the land. Only after these conditions are fulfilled and maintained can the individual Cambodian participate in the market free of state involvement.

And that's not all. Liberating individuals to act on their own is not sufficient to create the efficient land market desired by LMAP. There remains the vexing reality of transaction costs. When we are reminded that Demsetz's five assumptions will never be true even in advanced societies, creating a self-regulating land market in Cambodia becomes seemingly impossible, but once we remember that second-best approximations can be functional substitutes, there are reasons for optimism. The Torrens system on which the Cambodian Land Law is based works well enough in Australia to be widely adopted elsewhere. It is true that Australia enjoys first-world attributes that least-developed countries lack, but Cambodia has countervailing advantages: a legal *tabula rasa*, virtually unlimited foreign expertise, a powerful and enthusiastic government partner, and adequate funding. So, why not Cambodia?

THE IMPLEMENTATION PROCESS

Before we turn to the two case studies for a partial answer to that not so rhetorical question, some knowledge of the background against which they took place is necessary. An initial point is that the emphasis of land policy has been on investment and Economic Land Concessions (ELCs), rather than on landlessness and Social Land Concessions (SLCs). While ELCs have been created for various purposes throughout the country, the welfare function of the reforms remains largely aspirational. To the extent that local governments have resettled informal urban residents, it has largely been ad hoc and in response to displacement for economically motivated projects that have exacerbated, not alleviated, landlessness. Therefore, while SLCs may promise an orderly mechanism for addressing the property needs of poor Cambodians, the promise remains largely unfulfilled. As one NGO reported, "not a single [SLC] has been completed in accordance with the relevant laws." Rather, they "have perversely been used to steal land from the poor rather than provide it to them."[25]

[25] LICADHO, *Land Grabbing & Poverty in Cambodia: The Myth of Development*, (Phnom Penh: LICADHO, 2009) available at www.licadho-cambodia.org/reports/files/134LICADHOREportMythofDevelopment2009Eng.pdf. As with the failure to update registries, the likelihood that centralized cadastral registries would provide opportunities for insiders rather than

ELCs also have their issues, an initial one being the opacity of the process: "What has been agreed commercially in dozens of deals in every investment sector is regarded by Phnom Penh as confidential, despite the fact that the government is often selling or leasing public assets."[26] On the other hand, the private sector complains that connected individuals move onto land that they know is about to be included in an ELC so they can gain relocation compensation. Another indicator of corruption or at least strategic thinking is that ELCs are apparently politically timed. Many concessions have been issued immediately following an election but few before, implying that they are timed to avoid the negative press that frequently accompanies them. The degree of irregularity, however, is difficult to pin down. One human rights activist complained that the lack of adequate notice and an effective means of opposition meant that the government could indiscriminately grant land to private companies whenever the affected community was small and politically weak. A representative from the private sector, on the other hand, voiced concerns that unjustified negative press "painted all companies in an area with the same brush" and can lead Western investors sensitive to issues of corporate social responsibility to avoid the Cambodian market entirely in favor of Vietnam or Thailand.

The Boeung Kak Lake Case Study

Boeung Kak Lake lies in the heart of Phnom Penh and, like all of the city, was a virtual ghost town at the end of the Khmer Rouge regime. During the 1980s, however, former residents returned and were joined by refugees from border areas where fighting continued, and by 1991 the land around the lake was almost fully occupied. In fact, political parties seeking votes in Cambodia's first election encouraged housing development, and most residents had some documents of various origins purporting to be proof of ownership including "the issuance of house numbers, family books, small infrastructure improvements and the official witnessing of land sale contracts." In the late 1990s, the area saw an influx of foreign tourists, notably backpackers, and many guest houses were built around the lake and also on stilts above the water. Ancillary services – restaurants, bars, markets, construction firms – sprang up. By 2000,

the intended beneficiaries to profit could have been anticipated. The French Development Agency White Paper notes that land rights are "often manipulated during land registration operations to exclude legitimate rights holders in favour of local and national 'elites'." French Development Agency, 61.

[26] Robert Carmichael, "Conflicts Simmer Over Land Concessions," *Phnom Penh Post*, April 14, 2010.

the whole lake area "had been intensely settled, and many properties had been improved by their owners." In surveys taken a year later nearly 70 percent of residents said they wanted to stay and be able to upgrade their homes.[27]

The governmental encouragement notwithstanding, this settlement took place against a backdrop of legal uncertainty. As a "natural lake," the lake itself was clearly state public land, but its banks above the dry season water line were state private land and hence by statute available for formal titling. There were also nearby railroad lines, now informally occupied, which would normally be state public land and hence unavailable for titling, but the railroad had not operated for many years so that its status as public land may have lapsed. It also appeared that the railway authorities had encouraged their workers to settle on nearby land in the 1980s and granted them documents confirming that allocation. Finally, there were still other parcels that had apparently been used as parks and a zoo and were therefore, *prima facie*, state public land, but they had never been surveyed and registered as such, putting their tenure category into doubt. These circumstances led the Inspection Panel to conclude "that the land in question is state private land until an adjudication process can resolve competing claims by the State, existing possessors, or other claimants."[28]

With the above qualifications, therefore, most residents of the area as of the Land Law's 2001 promulgation had reason to be optimistic about the prospects of receiving formal title. They had lived in the area for years, developed the land, and created businesses and a community, constituting precisely the type of economic and social interests that LMAP was created to serve. Those prospects improved further with a series of auspicious events: In 2003, the government announced a massive upgrading of informal settlements in the Phnom Penh area; in 2004 it opened an international design competition specifically for the area, which stipulated that occupants would receive improved land and housing around the lake; and in 2006 the municipality of Phnom Penh announced that LMAP would begin systematic titling of the area.

Residents prepared to file claims for recognition, but the process never began. Initially, titling was denied on the ground that the area was state public land. Then the whole project fell apart when the government announced on February 6, 2007, that it had signed a 99-year lease for US$79 million with the politically connected real estate developer Shukaku, Inc., for 133 hectares of land, including the lake, which was to be partly filled despite its status as state public land. Then on August 7, 2008, the government approved a Sub-Decree converting the area to state private land and providing legal cover

[27] For original full text, see paragraphs 84 and 85 of World Bank, *Inspection Panel Report*.

[28] World Bank, *Inspection Panel Report*, paragraph 88.

for its commercial development, now marketed as Phnom Penh City Center, The Pearl of Cambodia.[29]

Pressure to leave began immediately, and a final eviction notice was issued by the Municipality of Phnom Penh in April, 2009. Residents were given three options: a lump sum of US$8,500 as total compensation for their property; a "dwelling unit" at a relocation site more than 20 km outside of the city and US$500 to cover moving expenses; or replacement housing in Boeung Kak, if residents moved first to a relocation site for four years while the new housing was constructed. No one trusted the developers to honor the promise of eventual permanent housing, so the real choice was between accepting compensation and finding substitute housing on one's own or moving to a distant relocation center. The US$ 8,500 figure was woefully inadequate, perhaps as far from full compensation as the amount awarded Japanese landlords. Market values in the area were estimated at US$ 3,000 a square meter, indicating that a modest plot of 50 m^2 would command a market value of $150,000 excluding the value of any structures or business good will. Since many residents possessed larger plots, often with multiple improvements, the real choice was between finding the vastly greater resources to purchase a similar site nearby or rebuilding their lives and livelihoods on the periphery of the city.

Most left, but they did not leave quietly. While many reported that they felt unable to protest because of fear of police and developer harassment and government retaliation,[30] the community did file a complaint with the Cadastral Commission, as well as applying to the judiciary for an injunction to postpone the eviction until a decision was made on its legality. The court denied jurisdiction, as did the court in our next case study, and ruled that the matter should be resolved by the Cadastral Commission.[31] It is not only Chinese courts, it appears, that know when a land dispute is too hot to handle.

Unlike Chinese farmers, however, Boeung Kak Lake residents had an alternative: the court of public opinion, in the form of international NGOs and the World Bank. On September 4, 2009, a Geneva-based NGO submitted a Request for Investigation on behalf of unnamed residents. The "Requesters," as the petitioners in the process are known, made a range of claims, including: (1) that government manipulation of tenure categories denied them the

[29] World Bank, *Inspection Panel Report*, paragraph 92.

[30] Many of them or their spouses worked for the municipality and feared that they could also lose their jobs as well as their homes. Residents also reported that "the police and company staff harassed them continually in order to weaken resistance and some were forced to demolish their homes themselves, despite being unable to stop crying." World Bank, *Inspection Panel Report*, paragraph 100.

[31] World Bank, *Inspection Panel Report*, paragraphs 97–101.

adjudication of their property as stipulated by the Land Law; (2) that the project failed to formalize their possession despite the clear requirement to do so; (3) that because of these failings, LMAP not only did not provide the promised enhanced security of formal title but actually weakened their preexisting tenure; and (4) that the situation in Boeung Kak Lake was repeated in other LMAP projects throughout Cambodia. Although the panel found that each of these claims was supported by its investigation and analysis, it is the third and fourth that deserve our attention here.

Had the World Bank's goal been solely to increase investment through the provision of clear property rights, one might argue that the third claim would have been beside the point. After all, transferring property rights from less to more productive users is the holy grail of neo-institutional economics. When transaction costs prevent a market exchange, as they did between the Pennsylvania Coal Company and downstream riparian owners, it is appropriate for the government to award the right to the entity that will use it more efficiently, and in this instance Shukaku was arguably more likely to develop Boeung Kak Lake more productively than individual residents who were still without formal title. Of course, in the best of all possible worlds, the residents would have received full compensation, but as the enclosures and *Sanderson* have illustrated, the process cannot always be voluntary or straightforward, or, to put it in Karl Polanyi's terms, sometimes a revolution of the rich against the poor is exactly what is needed to accelerate growth. Furthermore, manipulating the legal system to effectuate the transfer, as Cambodian officials did with the adroit shifting of residents' land from its original category of state private land to state public land to avoid systematic titling and then back to state private land to allow commercial development, is arguably no worse than Judge Clark's use of "natural" in *Sanderson*.

The problem with this scenario is not simply its cold-blooded injustice, but also its ignoring of LMAP's goal of alleviating poverty by securing poor Cambodians' access to land. To admit that a flagship land titling project exacerbated tenure insecurity would have been difficult even if blame could have been placed narrowly on the Bank's Phnom Penh employees, but the implications were broader because land formalization programs were under more general attack. The Requestors' fourth claim extended the problems to the rest of LMAP's Cambodian project; there had already been a Request for Investigation filed on similar grounds in Panama;[32] and media, NGO, and

[32] See World Bank, The Inspection Panel, Investigation Report No 56565-PA, Panama: Land Administration Project (Loan No. 7045-PAN), September 16, 2010. This report did not find Bank-specific mismanagement as the Cambodian report did, but it noted similar problems with titling programs, especially as they affect indigenous groups.

academic criticism against "land grabs" in developing countries was putting the whole titling enterprise under global scrutiny.[33]

Given these circumstances, it is understandable that the Report's eventual language is less straightforward in its affirmation of the Requestors' claims than the Report's own evidence might have justified. Nonetheless, the Panel faced the music and did its job. It first noted that "the degree of security provided by traditional, customary or other non-formal land tenure systems, especially in urban areas, has declined substantially since the early 1990s" and that "critical weaknesses in both design and implementation" had resulted in "the arbitrary exclusion of lands from the titling process [which] denied residents, especially the poor and vulnerable, the opportunity to claim and formalize their preexisting rights ... under LMAP." The lesson to be taken from this failure was stark, if tempered by bureaucratic caution: "land titling in itself cannot be expected to realize such diverse social and economic policy objectives in a range of contexts." Titling, the Report continued, had proved effective where there was little competition for land and hence few disputes, but ineffective, even counterproductive, "in increasing tenure security ... where the increase in land values is significant and where this may attract predatory interest."[34]

The final sentence deserves elaboration. The Panel found that land titling is effective only where *not* needed to determine ownership. While formal titles can enhance access to credit, this benefit seems hardly worth the expense of LMAP, especially if, as the Panel also concluded, this benefit will likely disappear should the titled land become worth stealing or the clarity of the registry be lost by widespread failure to record transfers. And that is the good news; the bad news comes in the second half of the sentence: "tenure security" is often *weakened* by titling where land is or becomes valuable. Put simply, LMAP had destroyed the property rights of the poor and weak and transferred them to the rich and connected.

When we remember that this finding comes from the premier institution known to promote such programs, this conclusion is deeply disturbing, but before we attempt a more general judgment of Cambodia's land regime, we must note that the Boeung Kak Lake story may not be representative of ELCs under the Land Law. Big money was at stake. When 133 hectares of prime real estate in the center of a nation's capital and largest city become available, self-dealing, public-private collusion, and political payoffs may be the norm

33 See, e.g., Center for Human Rights and Global Justice, *Foreign Land Deals and Human Rights: Case Studies on Agricultural and Biofuel Investment* (New York: New York University School of Law, 2010). See generally, Saskia Sassen, *Expulsions: Brutality and Complexity in the Global Economy* (Cambridge, US: Harvard University Press, 2014).

34 For original full text, see World Bank, *Inspection Panel Report*, paragraphs 256, 263, and 294.

everywhere, even in that bastion of rule-of-law propriety, the United States.[35] We turn, therefore, to a more typical instance of the use of the new law, the creation of the Koh Kong Sugar Plantation in rural southwest Cambodia, an area barely known even to the most intrepid Australian backpackers.

The Koh Kong Sugar Plantation Case Study

As with Boeung Kak Lake, we rely primarily on the work of an official investigation that invited, recorded, and analyzed not only the arguments of the aggrieved but also the submissions and counterarguments of those accused.[36] In this instance, instead of a World Bank Inspection Panel, the tribunal was the National Human Rights Commission of Thailand responding to a January, 2010, complaint filed by a coalition of Cambodia-based international NGOs led by the Community Legal Education Center (CLEC) on behalf of hundreds of households in three villages of Sre Ambel District, Koh Kong Province. The gravamen of the complaint was that the Khon Kaen Sugar Industry Public Company Limited, a Thai agribusiness company, had joined with Cambodian politicians and Taiwanese investors to use an ELC to dispossess the complainants of land and usufruct rights in violation of Cambodia's Land Law.[37]

According to the complainants, numerous third-party investigations, and the Human Rights Commission's Findings Report of March 2015, the project was illegal from its inception.[38] In March 2006, the Cambodian Cabinet approved the creation of two adjoining ELCs of close to 10,000 hectares each to the Koh Kong Sugar Industry Company and the Koh Kong Sugar Plantation Company. Although ostensibly separately owned by Cambodian nationals, both grantees were subsidiaries of Kohn Kaen and the clear intent

[35] For a detailed account of the less than arms-length interaction between government and developer arguably necessary to bring large scale real estate projects to fruition, see the trial court's rejection of the Manhattanville development in New York City, *Kaur* v. *New York State Urban Dev. Corp.*, 2009 NY Slip Op 08976 (December 3, 2009). The New York Court of Appeals reversed in *Kaur* v. *New York State Urban Dev. Corp.* 2010 NY Slip Op 05601 (June 24, 2010).

[36] National Human Rights Commission of Thailand, *Findings Report No. 115/2558*, March 10, 2015.

[37] The Complainants alleged and the Commission recognized a wide range of non-property rights violations including forced evictions, loss of educational and employment opportunities, child labor, and physical injuries, based on an equally wide range of Thai, Cambodian, and international norms beyond the 2001 Land Law that is the focus of our attention. See *Findings Report*, 3.1 "Types of Human Rights Violations and Resulting Damage" (pp. 5–8) and 4 "Relevant Laws, International Covenants and Guiding Principles" (pp. 20–6).

[38] The following account has been simplified for clarity's sake. The full chronology is available at *Findings Report* 3.1.1 Timeline (pp. 2–5).

was to combine the 18,641.6 total hectares (approximately 46,064 acres) in violation of the Land Law's limitation of ELCs to 10,000 hectares each.

Pressure on residents to leave began even before the formal signing of the ELCs in August, 2006, and the required notice and public hearings, environmental assessment, etc., were never held. The residents resisted and by the next March had taken their protest to Phnom Penh, prompting the Ministry of the Interior to convene meetings among aggrieved farmers, company representatives, and the CLEC. There followed years of negotiations, recommendations, fruitless appeals to local courts,[39] partial compensation, the departure of resigned and intimidated villagers, and eventually CLEC's complaint to the Thai Commission.

The illegality went beyond the procedural failures and the evasion of the 10,000-hectare limitation and gutted the core of the Land Law's purported goal: the recognition and clarification of Cambodians' property rights. Titling under the Law, one must remember, allowed all those in open and legal possession of land for the five years prior to 2001 to apply for formal title. Even more than the Boeung Kak Lake residents, the farmers of Sre Ambel fully satisfied this criterion. Most had been there since the end of the Khmer Rouge regime and some as far back as seventy years,[40] so the destruction of their rights was in direct defiance of the law. And it was not only possession that was lost. The concessions included four different types of land: highly fertile highlands suitable for such crops as corn, cassava, watermelon, and orchard crops such as cashews; floodplain land suitable for pasturage and rice cultivation; residential land; and forests. The last were used for pasturage and for gathering a variety of products including various vines, rattan, rubber oil, honey, various fruits, and herbs that villagers used for household items such baskets, charcoal, and traditional medicine but that they also sold in town markets.[41]

39 The *Findings Report* stated [p. 6] the following regarding the Cambodian judiciary's response:

> On this issue of alleged illegal land concession agreement between the companies and the Cambodian government, 220 households filed a lawsuit at Koh Kong Court in 2007, claiming that citizens were not informed and had no opportunity to participate in the land concession process. Afterwards, the companies attempted to negotiate and compensate citizens who filed the lawsuit. In 2009, 12 plaintiffs agreed to withdraw from the lawsuit, leaving 203 households still in litigation. In 2013, following the lead of the Boeung Kak Lake court, the Koh Kong Court ended the litigation process and transferred the case for review by the Cadastral Commission. This agency has a mechanism for managing certain types of land dispute, as part of the state mechanism for land management. According to Koh Kong Court, this case is beyond the jurisdiction of the court because villagers had no land titles.

40 *Findings Report*, 3.3.4(2) [17].

41 Ibid. 3.3.4(3) [17].

Even when villagers were able to retain residential land and some farmland, their livelihoods were substantially affected.[42] The Commission found that the average value of rice production for affected households decreased from 21,904 to 8,322 Thai baht, that orchard yields decreased overall from almost 2,087,291 to 45,522 baht and were completely eliminated in one of the three villages, and that the total value of livestock dropped by 28 percent. The loss in income was exacerbated by an increasing cost of living and the transformation of many residents from independent farmers to part-time agricultural laborers. Because of low wages and the seasonal nature of the work, others left the area for work in Phnom Penh or Thailand.[43]

Like their urban counterparts at Boeung Kak Lake, the villagers had lost their way of life, but for our immediate purposes what is most relevant is not what was lost but how it was lost and, most importantly, the role that formal law played. While it is clear that the Land Law failed to protect both groups, can we go further to say that it actually contributed to their dispossession? We address this contra-factual question in the next section, but to enable that inquiry, let's first look at the role of formal law in the two Koh Kong ELCs and specifically the mobilization of legal rhetoric by the defendants in the Thai Commission's proceedings. It is one of the great advantages of such third-party investigations by entities like national governments and the World Bank that the accused have not only the right but also the obligation to defend their actions. As we will see, they often do so by reference to law.

The initial appeal to law was the justification of a single 18,000 hectare plantation by Kohn Kaen's statement that its two subsidiaries "are 2 distinct business entities."[44] Of more interest is the repeated reference to law to excuse a range of illegal company actions. Once the concessions were established, in other words, law became part of the legitimation of the dispossession. A few examples from the defendant's defense will illustrate:[45]

> ¶1.1 [The company] was granted rightful land concessions by the Cambodian government on August 2, 2006. The project conducted a survey jointly with community leaders and government officials. Compensation was negotiated for affected villagers, according to proof of land possession.

[42] These figures are taken from the detailed compilation at *Findings Report*, 3.3.4 (5.1), "Loss of land and crop yield."

[43] *Findings Report* ¶5 Statement and Resolution of the Subcommittee on Community Rights, ¶5.1 Summary of Findings, ¶5.1 (2.1) at page 29.

[44] *Findings Report* 3.2 Statement of the Defendant, 3.2 (1.2) Statement to the Subcommittee on Civil and Political Rights, at page 9–10.

[45] Ibid. 3.2 (3) Written Statement, dated November 20, 2013, 3.2 (3.1.1–7), Illegal Possession of Villagers' Land, at page 11–12. Minor English errors have been corrected.

¶1.5 Approximately 200 households still claim that they have rights over the land concession area without any proof of land ownership or any relevant documents supporting their claims. As a result, the company cannot issue compensation and/or return the land. These villagers filed a lawsuit at Koh Kong Provincial Court.

¶1.6 After deliberations, Koh Kong Provincial Court ruled that villagers had no proof of rightful land ownership and returned this case to the Land Department of Koh Kong Provincial Office on August 30, 2012. Nevertheless, the company continues to negotiate and compensate most villagers. There remain only about nine households who refuse to negotiate with the company ... These villagers still cannot show any proof for the Land Department to issue their land titles.

¶1.7 The company will gladly pay compensation or reparations, or even return the land, if villagers can provide rightful proof of land rights (this proof is necessary for the company to show to the Cambodian government). To date, these villagers still cannot provide such proof, but have submitted complaints to many organizations as evident in the news. As a foreign investor, the company has the duty to respect and abide by the laws of Cambodia. All land concessions are still owned by Cambodia. The company is merely leasing the land according to the concession agreement. When the concession agreement expires, the company will have to return all land concessions back to the Cambodian government. Therefore, the company cannot return or hand over any land to anyone rightfully, without the approval of the Cambodian government.

This defense amounts to, "The law made me do it!"[46] The point, of course, is not that the law even permitted, much less forced, the destruction of villagers' property rights and livelihoods. The Commission recognized, as did the World Bank Inspection Panel, that Article 30 of the 2001 Land Law gave the occupants the right to apply for title. Kohn Kaen's repeated assertions that villagers lacked "rightful proof of land rights," therefore, is irrelevant to whether they had legal rights to the land. Unfortunately, the sophistry of its legal arguments does not mean that the presence of the law did not, in practice, facilitate Kohn Kaen's actions. While the Thai Commission and international NGOs were not fooled, accounts of international sugar ELCs are replete with stories of illiterate villagers being assured by local officials that the

[46] For a strikingly similar response by another Thai sugar business, the Mitr Phol Group, see www.mitrphol.com/index.php/en/csr/index.html, cited in Equitable Cambodia and Inclusive Development International, *Bittersweet Harvest: A Human Rights Impact Assessment of the European Union's Everything But Arms Initiative in Cambodia* (2013), 35.

law required their relocation, that their possession was illegal because they did not have the "relevant documents," that the land was therefore state property, and that the sugar companies would only compensate them if they immediately vacated and accepted whatever was offered.[47]

ASSESSING THE CONTRA-FACTUAL

Let us assume, however tentatively, that the Thai Commission Report strengthens the conclusion of the World Bank that land titling proved effective only where unnecessary. Add the conclusion that security previously provided by "traditional, customary or other non-formal land tenure systems" had declined substantially, and we have a dreary portrait of the state of land law reform in Cambodia. And Cambodia, unfortunately, is not alone. As Daniel Fitzpatrick and others have found in titling programs across the developing world,[48] far too often externally sponsored efforts to rationalize tenure systems in the developing world have had similar results. Sources as diverse as James Scott and the French Development Agency have long pointed out that the best laid plans often fail when ideology meets the reality of life in poor countries. When the ideology is alien and imposed by foreign powers, the chances of success decline further.

And yet the foreign experts forge on. They assume that the issuance of transparent, secure, and universally intelligible titles to poor and unsophisticated land holders will enable them to enter and thrive in the global market economy by mortgaging, improving, or selling their land. Occasionally it works. When a muddle of informal, legally invalid documents backed by years of occupancy and strong community relationships, which might be summarized as Geertzian local knowledge, is accurately and seamlessly replaced by a government certificate provided by competent honest bureaucrats and registered on a computerized cadastral map in the capital city, good things can happen. Such has apparently been the case in early systemic titling under LMAP where owners have enjoyed enhanced access to credit; titling in Peru has led to increased labor participation and school attendance, if not access to credit; and "big property" in Shenzhen has a significantly higher value than equivalent land with only small property rights.

Alas, what happens on a micro level to individual owners is not always replicated when whole societies are the target. Instead of the expected sanitized

47 For a series of detailed accounts of the operation of such schemes, see a focus group discussion held by Equitable Cambodia, *Bittersweet Harvest*, 51.

48 Daniel Fitzpatrick, "Evolution and Chaos in Property Rights Systems: The Third World Tragedy of Contested Access," *Yale Law Journal* 115 (2006): 996, 1012.

marketplace of zero transaction costs, there is ignorance and confusion. Local knowledge is supplanted by documents that the recipients cannot read and do not understand. Instead of competent and honest bureaucrats, occupants are visited by company representatives backed by corrupt local officials asking for their thumbprints on unintelligible pieces of paper in return for little or no compensation and backed, not by computerized databases, but by armed thugs. Preexisting occupants, even those with clear legal rights to ownership as in Boeung Kak Lake and Sre Ambel, are transformed from subsistence farmers or small merchants into manual laborers, often for the very company that displaced them.

But if we are interested in the role of property rights in development more generally, we must go further. It does not necessarily follow that the hypocrisy, coercion, and injustice of our case studies were bad for economic growth any more than were the hypocrisy, coercion, and injustice described in earlier chapters. To answer this question we must consider the contra-factual possibility that the Land Law had never been created and speculate on what would have happened in Cambodia's land market if the legal status of residents like those in our case studies had been left ambiguous. Would Shukaku and Khon Kaen Sugar Industry Public Company Limited have found a way to aggregate the land necessary for the Pearl of Cambodia and the export powerhouse of the Koh Kong plantation? Would the individual owners have done so on their own? Or would Boeung Kak Lake and Sre Ambel have remained a haven for backpackers and subsistence farmers respectively and, if so, would that have meant less economic growth?

Neither of our two official reports is of much help here. They are concerned with what happened: what went wrong with LMAP and whether Kohn Kaen violated human rights norms, not with an imaginary world without the Land Law, systematic and sporadic titling, and ELCs, much less the abstract questions of the value of titling programs per se or the role of property rights more broadly. That said, the evidence produced by their investigations provides grounds for addressing the broader question, and doing so can give us an additional perspective on the role of property rights developed in this book's other chapters.

We start with the question of whether the Land Law provided the legal cover necessary for the Phnom Penh government to lease the 133 hectares to Shukaku and the 18,000 to Kohn Kaen. Both concessions were illegal, so we are speculating that the very existence of a law enabled its violation. We cannot be certain, but several factors suggest that it would have been exceedingly difficult for the Phnom Penh government to take the land without the law. First, the residents had strong reason to believe that they had a *right* to the land. The Boeung Kak Lake residents had multiple quasi-official documents allowing them to possess the land, and the Sre Ambel farmers had used the land for generations without any indication from local or central officials that their occupation was anything but encouraged. Both groups had made substantial improvements to the land and participated in open and growing market economies, and both communities were cohesive enough to take collective action in their own defense. Each of these factors not only contributed to the residents' sense of entitlement and hence their willingness to resist, but they are also evidence of social capital, political power, and personal and community networks that might have made resistance effective if Shukaku, Kohn Kaen, and their political patrons had not been able to cloak themselves in the legitimating magic of rule-of-law rhetoric reinforced by the apparent omnipotence and omniscience of foreign experts.

If we assume, therefore, that absent the obfuscating function of the Land Law, the residents would have retained possession, can we further conclude that overall economic growth would have decreased? The tentative conclusion from the enclosures and nineteenth-century America is that the destruction of inefficient property rights accelerated growth, but the discussion in Chapter 5 of Chinese growth without clear property rights gives reason to pause. Perhaps Shukaku would have found a way to acquire enough lakeshore property to create the Pearl of Cambodia without the authority of an ELC by gradually aggregating individual properties or, less attractively, simply relying on the client-patron relationships that animate Cambodian politics and markets. Or, conversely, the myriad small merchants might have collectively produced equivalent wealth on their own, as did the urban villagers of Shenzhen and the TVEs of Shuang and Hancun. Either hypothetical situation would make a happier story than the injustice of the reality, but we must keep in mind that Shenzhen's small property rights buildings are still worth substantially less than fully legal real estate of equivalent quality. When Shukaku begins to market its luxury condominiums, by contrast, they will fetch top dollar, not some discounted amount because of the ambiguity of their legal pedigree.

More fundamental, however, is the question whether functioning markets would have emerged at all, whether, in other words, Cambodia would have been able to replicate the order without law that formed the basis for China's unprecedented growth. There is reason for pessimism. The vitality of both small property and TVE markets were dependent on social and institutional frameworks that may not exist in Cambodia. There is a huge disparity in the relative strength of the two countries' formal institutions, the local governments and Communist Party bureaucracies of China compared to those of the Municipality of Phnom Penh, the local governments in Sre Ambel, and the Cambodian People's Party. It is not just the formal structures. Cambodia has much lower levels of education, commercial sophistication, governmental legitimacy, and social capital than China, which may mean that the elaborate arrangements that created and sustain China's informal markets would not have been available to either individual residents or to Shukaku and Kohn Kaen. Without the social networks and structures that allowed institutions like local banks, law firms, and different levels of local government to cooperate in Shenzhen and elsewhere in China, it is likely that the legal form of an Economic Land Concession, even when deployed in direct violation of the Land Law, was necessary to provide the legitimacy and authority needed not only to force the residents to leave but also to convince Shukaku and Kohn Kaen to buy the concessions. It is the Land Law, after all, that enables Cambodian authorities to say – truthfully – to both domestic cronies and multinational corporations that their investments will be protected by clear, conclusive, and secure property rights.

Stepping back from the perspective of specific transactions, we can also speculate – still in our hypothetical mode – that similar dispossession of the relatively weak to encourage large scale investment will accelerate Cambodian growth. However charming the images of American, Austrian, and Australian backpackers enjoying cheap and congenial lodging and independent farmers entering the forest to gather rattan for baskets, they may not match the GDP production of high-rise condos full of expat lawyers and scores of freighters full of raw sugar headed to the European Union.[49] From the perspective of economic growth, therefore, we can tentatively conclude that it is possible that the Land Law may have done its job, however perversely.

If we expand the metric for success to include development more broadly, however, the picture becomes even more complicated. We must then weigh the glossy images of the Pearl of Cambodia and rising sugar exports against Amartya Sen's definition of development, one that values governmental

49 But they might, especially in agriculture. Hans P. Binswanger, Klaus Deininger, and Gershon Feder, in *Power, Distortions, Revolt, and Reform in Agricultural Land Relations*, World Bank Working Paper WPS 1164 (July 1993) argue that political power and corruption of the type endemic to Cambodia have prevented the higher potential productivity of small farms from being vindicated by market transactions. The result, according to them and consistent with the appearance of corporate "land grabs" in Cambodia and similar developing countries, is the concentration of land in the hands of multinational corporations. *See* Smita Narula, "The Global Land Rush: Markets, Rights, and the New Politics of Food," *Stanford Journal of International Law* 49 (2013) 101. In other words, the individual farmers may have collectively produced as much wealth as their large-scale corporate successors. When we remember, however, the dramatic increase in sugar exports and the concomitant benefits of participation in global markets, access to foreign exchange, and the import of agricultural technology, etc., this vision, as normatively attractive as it is, seems less plausible.

legitimacy, social trust, political development, bureaucratic competence, control of corruption, and the expansion of individual capabilities as ends in themselves as well as instruments for economic growth. It is difficult to imagine the events in our two case studies being anything but destructive of both these prerequisites to a successful society and even, if we lower our sights a bit, of the normative legitimacy identified by North and Demsetz as necessary for effective market institutions. The argument that transferring the property rights of the poor and unorganized to more resourceful and entrepreneurial actors will eventually make everyone richer is, therefore, a lot harder to sustain when we move beyond GDP to broader measures of success.

As we stated at the outset, however, comparing the messy reality of a very poor country with a utopian dream of clear property rights readily exchangeable in perfect markets seems unfair even to those in thrall to the dream. It may only exacerbate that unfairness to replace the top-down, technocratic paradise of formalization with a romantic, bottom-up vision of rural communities with clearly articulable local knowledge that will lead to both maximum productivity and social justice. What we can be sure of is this: neither utopia is likely to appear in Cambodia or anywhere else any time soon.

7

Property Rights and Social Change

In 1951, before neo-institutional economics, before law and development, and at the dawn of the concept of economic development itself, the United Nations identified the crux of the problem facing all societies hoping to advance:

> There is a sense in which rapid economic progress is impossible without painful adjustments. Ancient philosophies have to be scrapped; old social institutions have to disintegrate; bonds of caste, creed and race have to burst; and large numbers of persons who cannot keep up with progress have to have their expectations of a comfortable life frustrated. Very few communities are willing to pay the full price of economic progress.[1]

In the preceding chapters I have used case studies from the sixteenth to the twenty-first centuries to describe the role of property rights both in the scrapping of deeply rooted normative, behavioral, and institutional structures and, equally important, in the alleviation and legitimation of the concomitant social cost.

My goal has not been to provide precise answers to the pressing questions facing developing countries today. Human society is simply too complex for either abstract theory or a series of case studies to create the detailed roadmap that many understandably wish for, but some level of generalization from past experience is our only hope for understanding the process of rapid economic growth and social change.

[1] United Nations Department of Social and Economic Affairs, *Measures for the Economic Development of Underdeveloped Countries*, 1951. See also Michael J. Trebilcock, *Dealing with Losers: The Political Economy of Policy Transitions* (Oxford University Press, 2014). For a thorough discussion of the role of property rights in the bursting of bonds of caste, creed, and race, see Eduardo Moises Penalver and Sonia K. Katyal, *Property Outlaws: How Squatters, Pirates, and Protesters Improve the Law of Ownership* (New Haven: Yale, 2010).

To that end, in the next section I introduce two ideas from Joseph Schumpeter's *Capitalism, Socialism, and Democracy* to highlight common patterns from the diversity of the case studies and to understand why those patterns – recognized by the United Nations over sixty years ago – have eluded our contemporary understanding of the growth and development process. In the subsequent section, I focus on the different roles played by formal legal institutions in the deeply political processes described in the case studies. I then bring into the foreground what has been in the background of each narrative: whether the destruction of property rights in the pursuit of aggregate social benefit is legitimate, first in terms of the rule of law, then from a broader political perspective. I conclude with the implications of productive destruction of property rights for contemporary development practice.

INCESSANT REVOLUTION AND COMPARATIVE QUIET

Schumpeter's first idea is his famous description of capitalism as "the perennial gale of creative destruction ... that incessantly revolutionizes the economic structure *from within*, incessantly destroying the old one, incessantly creating a new one."[2] The case studies are concrete examples of such destruction and creation. Schumpeter's second idea is less well known but crucially important to understanding why mainstream discourse has rarely examined in detail the role of property rights in fundamental social change. In a footnote to his introduction of creative destruction and incessant revolution, Schumpeter made a sharp distinction between short- and long-term perspectives on the economy:

> Those revolutions are not strictly incessant; they occur in discrete rushes which are separated from each other by spans of comparative quiet. The process as a whole works incessantly however, in the sense that there always is either revolution or absorption of the results of revolution.[3]

[2] Joseph A. Schumpeter, *Capitalism, Socialism, and Democracy* (London: Routledge, 1943). Creative destruction is introduced in Chapter VII The Process of Creative Destruction, pp. 81–6. I have changed the order of the quote. The phrase "creative destruction" appears at 84, the rest at 83. Schumpeter had an even darker view of progress than the United Nations, believing that the very success of competitive capitalism would destroy the normative structures that sustained it, including the belief in private property and the willingness to defend it. As befits an economist who predated neo-institutional economics and attention to law, Schumpeter mentioned property and contract rights only in terms of the normative decay inherent in capitalism and law more generally not at all. See The Destruction of the Institutional Framework of Capitalist Society in Chapter XII Crumbling Walls at pp. 139–63.

[3] Schumpeter, *Capitalism*, 83, footnote 2.

Schumpeter thought that mainstream economists were too concerned with the periods of comparative quiet and not concerned enough about the process of change. He conceded that the investigation of the "existing structures" of a specific market at a specific time – pricing in a retail oligopoly, for example – may clarify the details of why one firm prospers and another stagnates. He insisted, however, that this clarification will be "meaningless" unless it can illuminate how such structures are created and destroyed, which does not occur through manipulation of the status quo but through "industrial mutation" forced on participants by fundamental changes like new markets, organizational innovations like the assembly line, or technological changes like the computer. The essential fact about capitalism for him was not how markets operate but how they are created, destroyed, and recreated.

I believe that Schumpeter's concern is as valid today with regard to the role of property rights as it was then for the functioning of markets generally. Observers of the contemporary development process – economists and lawyers alike – focus too much on the operation of stable markets and too little on how those markets must change for progress to occur. Even worse, they often substitute an idealized vision of property law derived from Western theory for the empirical reality of the markets – mostly non-Western markets – they are working to reform. As a result, when they do focus on change, they too seldom consider fully the process of transformation and fail to weigh adequately the frustration of legitimate expectations noted by the United Nations and caused by Schumpeter's "perennial gale." They focus on the end point of creation and neglect the vicissitudes and pain of the destruction necessary to get there.

To explain the nature and cost of this approach, this book has applied Schumpeter's long-term, dynamic perspective to the study of property rights and development. As he did with economic structures more generally, I acknowledge that the study of existing property rights can teach us how a given market works and how to make incremental improvements, but property rights in the development context have a special character that makes concentration on the present dangerous not only in terms of understanding development but also in achieving its goals: The faithful enforcement of "existing structures" can and indeed *will* maintain the status quo and protect the interests of those benefiting from existing institutions.

There is nothing inherently wrong with stability. None of the dispossessed of our case studies – from the English villeins and freemen barred from the commons to the Boeung Kak Lake hostel owners dispossessed by Shukaku – deserved to be displaced. Whether the sacrifice of property rights for growth can be justified in poor societies will be addressed in the next section, but in a just and wealthy society, the status quo may be worth protecting even in long-term, utilitarian terms. In fact, the comfort of their home societies and their own place therein may help to explain why development practitioners from the affluent world are so attracted to the strict enforcement of formal property rights. The continuity that may be in the best interest of the elites of the United States, Denmark, or Japan, however, may not be appropriate to the majority of the population of contemporary developing countries.

From the perspective of people at the bottom of the world hierarchy, therefore, economists and development practitioners should not be concerned with maintaining the formal rules that support existing structures. On the contrary, they should be searching for a way to replace the old property regimes with more productive ones, but they should do so while constantly being aware that creating the new requires the destruction of the old and that the cost of progress can be high. Otherwise, unless care is taken to minimize the pain and to prepare for new legitimate property structures, whatever gains may come from rapid economic growth will be at the mercy of political instability, and the most fundamental goals of human dignity and autonomy, social justice, and the rule of law may fade even further into the indefinite future. To assist in this difficult and complex task, the next section attempts to bring some order out of the case studies.

WHAT IS THE ROLE OF LAW?

One can imagine a number of underlying causes of the destruction of social structures. War, revolution, plague, climate change, and even moral revelation come to mind. Law, on the other hand, seems an unlikely primary driver of fundamental change, but as the narratives of the use, abuse, and absence of property law in the previous chapters attest, law can and often does play a significant instrumental, if not causal, role in how various societies have approached the dilemma of reform and preservation.

One commonality has been the presence of formal law. Even in the Chinese case, formal institutions, albeit not property institutions per se, were instrumental in creating the social structures that allowed economic growth. In our other chapters, it was formal property law itself. Law, lawyers, and courts appeared on all sides of the enclosure process. Legal devices like the lack of corporate identity allowed the court in *Gatewards* to ignore established property rights, but legal fictions like the presumption of a lost grant in *Wimbledon* slowed the process and occasionally stopped it. Similarly, we saw courts play both roles in the American water law cases, transforming natural flow in *Sanderson* to protect illegal pollution at one point but later sheltering absolute ownership of percolating water in *Bristor* long after environmental and economic forces would, and perhaps should, have replaced it with prior appropriation.

It is harder to find that double role in the Japanese case. If the narrow definition of absentee landlord and the landlords' dominance of the implementing Agricultural Committees had been maintained, it would undoubtedly have lessened the pain of the landlord class, but they did not survive, and when the Supreme Court was asked to enforce the constitutional requirements of public use and just compensation, it simply rubber-stamped the wholesale elimination of an entire social class. Everything is relative of course, and the parliamentary process leading to the Agricultural Land Law, the participatory nature of the Agricultural Committees, and the availability of Supreme Court review were highly preferable to the roughly contemporaneous violent dispossession of mainland Chinese landlords. But violence was not a likely approach for either the American military or the Japanese conservative parties. It may be more accurate instead to see the dominant role of law in the Japanese case not as softening the blow or slowing the process but as legitimating the conservative parties' decision to build their political base on independent farmers rather than on their erstwhile landlord allies.

The Cambodian land law reform is perhaps the most distinctive from the perspective of the role of formal law. It is also deeply ironic. It began as a self-conscious attempt to rationalize what Acemoglu and Robinson would likely consider an example of the "archaic forms of property rights" that they identified as obstacles to growth in *Why Nations Fail*, and in this sense is a manifestation of Schumpeterian processes in the contemporary development world. Although it is extremely unlikely that the Australian solicitors drafting the law were thinking of creative destruction per se, the Land Law and LMAP were an attempt to do precisely that: to replace existing community-based property structures with a more productive regime. Instead of relying on a potpourri of inconclusive documents from a variety of prior colonial, national, and local authorities backed up by evidence of decades of possession, Boeung Kak Lake hostel owners and Sre Ambel rice farmers would enter negotiations with international hotel chains and agribusinesses armed with transparent, unitary, and secure property rights that would have had the potential of getting them a better deal more quickly.

As it turned out, of course, only the destruction part worked as planned. A new regime was created and new markets exploited, but it was not the hostel owners and farmers who wielded the newly created property rights. As the World Bank and Thai Commission reports show, the law was at best ineffective where needed to protect existing property owners and frequently, if not regularly, played the predatory role that we saw with Boeung Kak Lake and the

Koh Kong plantation. As a result, it is even harder to see anything "rule-of-law-like" in the implementation of Cambodia's Land Law than in the superficially more informal and manipulative narratives of the other case studies.

If we generalize from these accounts of law – or at least of legal form – in action, an initial observation is that even when we encounter property law and property rights, they are rarely playing the protective role we would expect from conventional wisdom. On the contrary, they are facilitating or legitimating the destruction of existing structures and, if we adopt an optimistic view of Schumpeter's perennial gale, creating more productive ones. The *Bristor* litigation is the obvious exception. As in the other examples, it occurred at a time of economic pressure on existing structures, but the Arizona Supreme Court ultimately chose the protective over the destructive role, and an analysis of the interests involved may give us deeper insight into why the protective role is so unusual in this context.

We begin with the parties. Bristor represented preexisting agricultural interests, Cheatham the newly arrived, fast-drilling cotton farmers who were using their established property rights to drain water from their neighbors' land. It was again old suing new, but with the twist that the old wanted changes to the law in order to preserve the economic status quo. Although there is nothing in the opinions or commentary explicitly saying so, we assume that the newcomers were using the water more profitably, if not more efficiently, than the old-timers. We can make this assumption because logic, buttressed by the Coase Theorem, tells us that existing well owners would have otherwise preserved their interests by paying the newcomers not to drill. If we accept this reasoning, therefore, we might interpret the reaffirmation of absolute ownership in *Bristor II* somewhat differently than we did in Chapter 3. Instead of attributing Chief Justice Stanford's reversal as folding under political pressure or as a come-to-Jesus conversion to a rule-of-law as a law-of-rules approach to the judicial role, we might interpret it as correctly decided from a utilitarian perspective: not only were the new wells protected by formal property rights, but they were also more valuable than the old ones.

That analysis would be incomplete and wrong, however, because it would repeat the frequent mistake of confounding profitability with efficiency and would also miss what is interesting and paradoxical about *Bristor II*. It was not solely the owners of nearby wells who were being harmed by the court's refusal to apply prior appropriation but also the future urban residents of Arizona. Mid-twentieth-century Arizona was not in one of Schumpeter's periods of comparative quiet, but about to enter the gale of creative destruction that would convert its economic structure from agriculture to the urban sectors of industry, recreation, and housing. If *Bristor I* had prevailed and Cheatham's absolute property right in the water below his fields destroyed and replaced with the prior appropriation regime that was eventually introduced thirty years later, this iteration of Schumpeter's incessant revolution would have followed its economic course, rather than being legally blocked. In this sense *Bristor II* echoed *Sanderson I–III* in representing not only doctrinal fealty but also in serving yesterday's interests.

The crucial difference was in the relative power of the contending parties, a fact that makes clear that the transaction costs-cutting role played by the judicial destruction of property rights is highly contingent. While it is impossible to gauge precisely the political forces behind change in the two situations, one difference is clear. The coal industry advocating the destruction of property rights in *Sanderson* was concentrated and well financed. It may have been looking forward to an even more prosperous future after the elimination of the threat of damages and injunction, but it was already an economic and political force to reckon with. The equivalent forces in *Bristor* were not. The owners of established wells were not without political and economic clout but they were only one segment of a divided agricultural sector. Their non-agricultural allies, the urban interests who would benefit most from a more regulated water regime, were just emerging if they existed at all. The future retirees, after all, were still a decade or more away from moving to Sun City. That imbalance was clear when Stanford reversed himself and *Bristor II* was decided. It became even clearer over the next few decades as environmental and urban interests remained unable to convert a broad but shallow consensus in favor of conservation into effective legislation.

It is not necessarily an uplifting view of law to claim that its role is to destroy legitimate social structures in order to usher in economic growth. It becomes even more difficult to defend a system in which a society's future depends on the strength of special interests' influence on the judiciary. The fickleness of judicial decision making is apparent in the contrast between *Wimbledon*, with its accomplished lawyer, and *Tollard Farnham* without one, but it is even more so in our two American cases: Should it matter whether it is the rock-hard Henry M. Hoyt or the wishy-washy Rawghlie Clemont Stanford representing efficiency and progress? The substantive misgivings are obvious and well-founded, but it does not necessarily follow that they carry the day when one remembers that the task at hand is nothing less than economic progress.

IS THE DESTRUCTION OF PROPERTY RIGHTS LEGITIMATE?

Contemporary neo-institutional economics is based on the premise that effective, if not perfectly efficient, property rights are essential to economic growth. If that is correct and if poor societies currently suffer from unproductive property rights, those existing structures must be changed. It may be most comfortable for us to imagine effective rights simply emerging through some undescribed consensual or undetectable evolutionary process, but that is a fantasy of bad economics. In actuality, there are real costs and real losers even as societies prosper. Once we recognize that even positive change will be hard, the roles of law described in our case studies may begin to look a little less unattractive, and we should ask whether they might be legitimate, warts and all. We start with the inevitable, and inevitably unsatisfying, discussion of how the roles of property law recounted herein comport with the rule of law.

Does It Violate the Rule of Law?

If there is any mantra more sacrosanct and more uncritically used in contemporary development discourse than secure property rights, it is the rule of law. As a result, using the standard vocabulary to address the topic even superficially is beyond the scope of this book. The concept is too capacious, too vague, too contested to use either as the baseline for evaluating or analyzing these case studies or the converse, i.e., to use the case studies to refine our understanding of the rule of law. The former would excessively narrow the focus of the book, which is not the study of property rights solely as law but also as constituent of social and economic structure. The latter – to attempt to say something original and significant about the rule of law in light of the pain of development – deserves its own book. That said, the centrality of the concept in development discourse requires some attention to the concerns that it raises.

Although any definition would be incomplete, "the rule of law, not men," amplified jurisprudentially by Scalia's *The Rule of Law as a Law of Rules*, will suffice, first to begin the discussion, then to illustrate its futility. This usage is perhaps the most common for laypersons, including most likely the economists and bureaucrats who design and implement law reform projects such as LMAP. It is also the one most obviously violated in our case studies. By its terms, only procedurally proper legislation can legitimately change citizens' rights and obligations, and *Gateward's*, *Sanderson*, and *Bristor I* are clearly illegitimate. Judges should not decide cases on any ground other than statutory and constitutional rules. A slightly looser version would include prior judicially created rules, but would, of course, immediately face the question of the original legitimacy of the earlier decision.

To state this definition, even its cartoon version, is to see its impossibility. First, words simply don't have meanings that are clear in all circumstances. Justice Clarke was not wrong in terms of popular usage when he said that the natural use of coal land was to mine coal, but he was wrong legally when he concluded that pollution was consistent with the natural flow doctrine. Everyone knew then and now that his use was dishonest, but judicial sophistry will usually not be so immediately apparent. "Natural" in the context of natural flow is fairly clear, especially compared to the many words in law that are empty of specific meaning. "Reasonable," "disproportionate," and "unfair" are three that legislatures repeatedly use precisely *because* they have no content, and there are phrases like "public use" and "just compensation" from the Japanese and American constitutions that, like "natural," may have a core meaning but that are so dependent on context that it becomes impossible to guarantee their consistent application as circumstances change. The list of such terms could go on indefinitely and, in the hands of skilled lawyers, perhaps forever. Then there is the effect of the passage of time and the concomitant change in the meanings of the words. Here we get to the public debate over American constitutional interpretation, but the basic issue is important in less contentious settings as well, and the correct interpretive approach just as uncertain. Even if one adopts originalism, furthermore, there is the difficulty of learning and applying a term used by drafters decades of centuries before in a socially, technologically, and politically quite distinctive society.

The "rule of law, not men" mantra is not only linguistically impossible, however. It would also preclude emulation of the common law system, the very family of legal systems that many neo-institutional economists most admire. We will therefore return to the rule of law and the ideal type of legal system for developing countries when we discuss the implications of the destruction of property rights for development practice in the final section, but now let's look at the process of creative destruction from a broader perspective.

Is It Politically Legitimate?

There are other forms of legitimacy than the rule of law. So, without deciding whether the roles of the courts in these various transitions were violations or vindications of the rule of law – one could argue either way – let's move to a more accessible objection to the destruction of property structures: political legitimacy. We begin with the outliers, China and Cambodia, both authoritarian regimes with weak judiciaries. When the Xiaogang commune leaders decided to contract with individual households, they had no legal or bureaucratic authority whatsoever. Their authority came from the same place as that of the actors in the other examples of China's economic policy initiatives described in Chapter 5, the institutional strength of the amalgam of the Chinese Communist Party and PRC government known as the

Party-State. As discussed in Chapter 5, there was nothing legal about these structural changes, at least if we use the conventional definition of the term. What these transitions, which have received wide popular support, do have is what is called performance legitimacy.[4] The Party-State enjoys legitimacy because it has delivered the goods for the Chinese people, not because it was elected, has created an independent judiciary, or embodies any particular ideology, whether Marxist-Leninist-Maoist thought, Confucian values, or liberal democracy.

Cambodia presents a different and anomalous picture. Law and rule of law rhetoric are everywhere and the law was the vehicle for the application of the new set of best-practices property rights, but the law, both on the level of the Land Law itself and as an overarching ideology, operated illegally to dispossess property owners, not vindicate their rights. It was the shifting back and forth from state public to state private land at Boeung Kak Lake and the demand for the "relevant documents" in Sre Ambel that provided the veneer of legality needed to evict the residents and deny them the rights expressly recognized by the statute itself. It is impossible, therefore, to consider the events recounted in Chapter 6 as legitimate by any normative metric, much less the rule of law.

Of course, most Cambodian farmers have not been displaced, if only because their land is not valuable enough to attract investors. It is possible that the titling program has thus provided some legitimacy to the Hun Sen regime, but if it is of benefit only when land is not valuable, that legitimacy likely disappears when the law facilitates the theft of valuable land. If so, it is unclear where any legitimacy will come from. The Hun Sen regime cannot fall back on either a democratic pedigree or the PRC's performance legitimacy. Of course, if the Pearl of Cambodia and the international sugar trade deliver the goods of economic growth despite, or perhaps because of, their violation of clear property rights, the hostel owners and subsistence farmers may be forgotten in the big picture of prosperity.

We now turn to the American cases. Even if we can't bring *Sanderson* and the like into the rule of law pantheon, one might defend judges' policymaking just as one defends legislatures': they were elected. Even with appointed federal judges, the iconic cases that have shaped American society, *Plessy* then *Brown*, *Roe*, *Citizens United*, etc., cannot be comfortably defended by reference to the definition of the rule of law used above. On the contrary, they are the direct result of the politicization of federal judicial selection via American

4 Stated succinctly by Xi Jinping himself on June 28, 2013: "If we fail to govern our party effectively or strictly ... sooner or later it will lose its standing for ruling the country and will be cast aside by history." Cited in Minxin Pei, *China's Crony Capitalism: The Dynamics of Regime Decay* (Cambridge: Harvard University Press, 2016), 256.

presidential elections. This does not, however, delegitimize them, for as President Obama, himself a constitutional law professor, put it, "Elections have consequences." But just because politicized judiciaries may be acting legitimately when destroying property rights in pursuit of economic growth, it does not mean that it is a good thing.

Is It Worth the Pain?

An initial issue is the possibility of error. Entrusting the destruction of existing economic structures to courts and judges assumes a policymaking competence that may not exist, but the judicial role takes on added weight when we remember what is at stake even if the decisions are correct in some utilitarian sense. The painful adjustments and frustrated expectations of those unable to adjust to the scrapping of ancient ways of life demand that we go slowly and, where possible, deliberatively. Whether the sacrifice of the ways of life of the contemporary equivalent of sixteenth-century villeins and freemen can be justified in terms of long-term aggregate benefit is a question that cannot be ignored or dispensed with by a self-serving admonition to poor states to redistribute any economic gains to compensate for the losses of the weak. Effective redistribution from the successful to those left behind simply will not happen. It did not happen in the enclosures or to the losers in nineteenth-century America or to the Japanese landlords, and it will not happen in Cambodia or similar least-developed countries.

In this context, it is imperative to remember that it was the courts' braking role, not their policy wisdom or doctrinal fealty that E. P. Thompson identified as "an unqualified human good," and we might once again reinterpret *Bristor II* in that light. Even if we are correct in our speculation that the decision blocked the economic, social, and environmental progress that would have occurred if absolute ownership had been immediately replaced with prior appropriation, the delay may have played the ameliorating function that Thompson celebrates. This argument is difficult in the instant case, of course, because we are not dealing with serfs and freemen or even unsuspecting members of the middle class like the Sandersons, but aggressive cotton growers, who were just as grasping and avaricious (or not) as their neighbors and likely had more money. It is thus very hard to see them as among those whose "expectations of a comfortable life" should be protected by postponing an inevitability that will have significant aggregate benefits.

But the economic successes of particular cases should not distract us from either the material or, equally important, dignitary cost to the losers when property rights are destroyed in the process of economic progress. Those costs and the multiple functional weaknesses of judicial interventions in such circumstances should make us question the wisdom of legal institutions acting as arbiters of our economic future unless there is solid political support, even when the judges are envisioning that future correctly. Of course, if a political consensus exists, judicial intervention may not be needed, but there will be times when it will be. It is those cases where the wisdom that may come from deliberation and humility can devise courses of action that will liberate the winners to propel the economy and society forward but simultaneously not leave the losers too far behind.

WHAT DOES THE NEED TO DESTROY PROPERTY RIGHTS MEAN FOR DEVELOPMENT PRACTICE?

If the narratives of the preceding chapters have succeeded in complicating our understanding of the role of property rights in economic growth, the inevitable question is whether our additional insight into the role of law in development can improve the practice of legal reform in today's poor countries. As I've emphasized throughout, I make no pretense of providing universal blueprints for long-term legal construction or immediate answers to pressing policy issues. The variety of experiences and circumstances both in the case studies and in today's world is too great. But two lessons emerge and I close by attending to them.

The Centrality of Definitions

The first lesson is definitional. Dani Rodrik, a neo-institutional economist who has argued consistently for a complicated and flexible approach to development, recently spoke at an American law school about the role of institutions in economic growth. After ninety minutes of listening to Rodrik refuse to give pat answers to the institutional needs of poor countries, a frustrated student got the last question: "Isn't there *anything* that you can say for sure is needed?" The answer, as the economist got up to leave: "Property rights." When asked the next day via email if he meant that fully articulated statutory property rights enforced by an honest, competent, and independent judiciary was what he meant, Rodrik answered no and explained that he was using "'property rights' as a short cut for any mechanism that ensures investors can appropriate returns to their economic activities."[5]

[5] Personal communication with the author.

The problem, needless to say, is that law students, law professors, and lawyers in general think in terms of formal institutions. They do not think of the networks of interpersonal relationships that gave security to the hostel owners around Boeung Kak Lake or to the farmers in Sre Ambel as property rights. Nor will they consider the interactions among formal and informal institutions that provide tenure security to owners of small property rights buildings in Shenzhen or reassure multinational corporations that their Chinese investments are safe as law. For legally trained people, law requires certain forms: legislatively or judicially created rules; courts with judges who announce their decisions openly and explain their reasoning; formal procedures to govern the adjudication process; and, even in American states with elected judiciaries, a significant degree of autonomy from straightforward political action and influence.

The rules may be hopelessly vague; the judges may be political hacks, corrupt cronies, or simply incompetent; the procedures may be obfuscating and unnecessary. But the forms must exist. Perhaps most fundamental, these rules and procedures must relate to a sovereign. Custom, however binding on the members of a group, is not law in our narrow but important usage until or unless it becomes customary law, i.e., custom recognized by the state. Of course, once custom, especially custom governing land, has been formalized to fit into the state machinery, it loses its customary nature, but it gains the forms and formality necessary for lawyers to recognize it as law and specifically as property rights.

The World Bank's Cambodian LMAP project was emphatically law. It may have been distorted by the Hun Sen regime to the point where it legitimated the dispossession of precisely the owners whose property rights it was intended to secure, and it may have been unenforced by Cambodian courts. It may have been, in other words, bad or ineffective law, but unless one takes the position that only law that operates as intended qualifies for the label, LMAP and the 2001 Land Law satisfy the requirements for legal professionals. Ironically, they may not satisfy the criteria for developmental economists on at least one level. For economists, "property rights" denotes not formal requirements but functionality, specifically the provision of security in ownership of economic assets. Here Cambodian law failed those whose preexisting tenure it was intended to secure.

On another level, however, perhaps the Land Law did satisfy both definitions, and here is where the paradox of titling programs becomes most acute. It is true, as the World Bank and the Thai Human Rights Commission recognized, that the Land Law destroyed both formal and informal claims of the residents of Boeung Kak and Koh Kong, but it did not leave the land in the legal limbo that titling programs have created elsewhere. The current claimants, Shukaku and Kohn Kaen, do not rely on a potpourri of documents or the proof of local knowledge. They have clear, unambiguous, registered ownership accessible from around the globe. More important, they have the political and economic power to defend those property rights against all comers, certainly against the previous owners, who have largely scattered in search of new lives. For them – and other wealthy and connected agribusinesses and real estate developers in Cambodia and elsewhere – the formality of the law may operate precisely as intended. With the ability to demonstrate to international hotel chains and construction companies that their investments are backed by a form of ownership utterly familiar to their general counsels, Shukaku's Phnom Penh City Center may well develop into The Pearl of Cambodia that its advertising promises that it will become.[6] Similarly Thai, Taiwanese, and other agribusinesses may continue or even accelerate the export of sugar and other commodities that has already contributed to Cambodia's impressive GDP growth. If these results materialize, both economists and lawyers will have the law they want – functional, formal, institutionalized, and enforceable.

The Value of Caution and Humility

A corollary to our definitional lesson is to be careful, very careful, and to assume that everything that can go wrong within a political and bureaucratic system will go wrong. The Kings Bench was not available to the farmers of Sre Ambel, whose rights to forage in neighboring forests were enclosed, and there is little reason to be optimistic about similar villages in other least-developed countries facing international agribusiness investment. Nor are such countries likely to have judiciaries with the institutional strength and legitimacy of the Pennsylvania or Japanese supreme courts. Indeed, institutions with even the perhaps lesser strength and legitimacy of the Chinese Communist Party may be difficult to find. This is not to declare all poor country bureaucracies and judiciaries corrupt and ineffective, but creating institutions that are capable, willing, and free to implement the dreams of first world planners is, to put it mildly, a challenge, and if one assumes competence and honesty where they do not exist, the result will often not simply be money and time wasted, but a situation on the ground that is worse than it was under the preexisting regime.

The task is made all the more difficult when the impetus, ideology, expertise, and money come in the form of short-term foreigners without the detailed

[6] For a marketing video, see New Development of Phnom Penh City Center The Pearl of Cambodia www.youtube.com/watch?v=FMv5ToQfVdQ. Not a mosquito in sight!

local knowledge and experience possessed by the domestic actors that dominated in all but our Cambodian case study. As long ago as 1792, Robespierre, in a speech in opposition to the call by his comrades to spread the French revolution by war, recognized the fundamental issue:

> The most extravagant idea that can be born in the head of a political thinker is to believe that it suffices for people to enter, weapons in hand, among a foreign people and expect to have its laws and constitution embraced. It is in the nature of things that the progress of reason is slow and no one loves armed missionaries; the first lesson of nature and prudence is to repulse them as enemies.[7]

Of course, World Bank economists and Australian solicitors do not come bearing literal weapons, but it would be a failure of imagination not to recognize iPads, cadastral mapping satellites, helicopters, and Land Rovers as the twenty-first-century equivalent of Napoleon's cannon. It is not simply that the technological, knowledge, and wealth gap between first-world reformers and third-world farmers or workers is overwhelming. Nor is it only a question of local knowledge. Even if we indulge in the contrafactual assumption that anthropologists could replace development lawyers and economists, the stark fact of foreignness would remain.

Of course, local political forces will be there to manipulate and exploit the foreign experts and spend their money, and the result can be the best of all possible worlds, arguably as it was with Japan's conservative parties and the Allied occupiers in the mid-twentieth century. But Japan was a thoroughly developed country, had already had been a democracy, and enjoyed strong institutions and enormous social and human capital. When the foreign influence is captured not by the Liberal Democratic Party but by the equivalent of Hun Sen and his cronies, however, any destruction of property rights in the name of economic growth is not likely to be as politically palatable. Nor is it likely to be as effective in the long run without the legitimacy that democracy, legal process, and institutional strength can deliver.

I do not mean to claim that democracy is necessary. No country has developed as a democracy, and it would be both arrogant and foolish to demand it of today's poor countries. What is necessary, however, are effective domestic institutions. Cambodia was the tenth fastest-growing economy in 2016,[8] but even performance legitimacy has its limits. In the medium term, it and similar temporarily fast-growing developing countries will need the institutional

7 https://en.wikiquote.org/wiki/Maximilien_Robespierre.

8 *CIA World Fact Book* www.cia.gov/library/publications/resources/the-world-factbook/rankorder/2003rank.html.

legitimacy that only their own population can create. It is in that sense, therefore, that twenty-first-century development practitioners resemble Napoleon. They must be warned that foreign expertise, good will, and money cannot substitute for the time consuming, incremental process of internally driven national construction. In the end, it is only home-grown institutions that can legitimate the pain that development will inevitably cause.

Index

For EU product safety concerns, contact us at Calle de José Abascal, 56–1°, 28003 Madrid, Spain or eugpsr@cambridge.org.

www.ingramcontent.com/pod-product-compliance
Lightning Source LLC
LaVergne TN
LVHW011519200926
848484LV00001B/80

* 9 7 8 1 1 0 8 4 2 2 8 3 3 *